The Rise and Fall of a Violent Crime Wave

Crack Cocaine and the Social Construction of a Crime Problem

The Rise and Fall of a Violent Crime Wave
Crack Cocaine and the Social Construction of a Crime Problem

Henry H. Brownstein
The University of Baltimore

DISCARD

Harrow and Heston
PUBLISHERS
Guilderland, New York

Copyright © 1996, Harrow and Heston, Publishers

Harrow and Heston, Publishers
1830 Western Avenue
Albany, N.Y. 12203

Library of Congress CIP:

Brownstein, Henry H.
The Rise and Fall of a Violent Crime Wave: Crack Cocaine and the Social Construction of a Crime Problem / Henry H. Brownstein
p. cm.
Includes bibliographical references and index.
ISBN 0-911577--36-X (alk. paper)

1. Drug abuse and crime--United States. 2. Violent crimes -- United states. 3. Crack (Drug) -- United States. I. Title.
HV5825.B78 1996
364.2'4--dc20

96-34878
CIP

Contents

List of Tables

List of Figures

Preface

The falling rate of violent crime in the United States in the early 1990s caught the attention and imagination of criminologists and criminal justice practitioners and policy-makers alike. As they watched the decline in violent crime statistics, they tended to forget the sharp rise that immediately preceded the dramatic fall. This book is about the wave of violent crime that washed over the U.S. between 1980 and 1994. It focuses on the social and cultural processes that contributed first to the rise and then to the fall of violent crime as it was observed and experienced in American cities.

The book is largely based on my experience as the government employee in New York State responsible for the generation of Uniform Crime Reports (UCR) statistics, and on my federally-funded research on the subject of drugs and violent crime. Material is also used from news reports and government documents—federal, state, and local—produced about "the drug problem" during the period under consideration.

From 1982 to 1995 I was an employee of the government of New York State. I began in 1982 as a Program Research Specialist responsible for the evaluation of alternative-to-incarceration programs. In 1985 I was promoted to Principal Program Research Specialist. While in that title I began working on joint projects with Narcotic and Drug Research, Inc. (later known as National Development and Research Institutes, Inc., NDRI in either case) in New York City as Co-Principal Investigator on a series of studies of the relationship between drugs and violence.

The first of the drugs and violence studies were based on police records and reports of the drug relatedness of homicides. These studies were funded by the National Institute of Justice. More recently this research has involved interviews with adults incarcerated and youth under custody in New York State for homicide or other violent or non-violent offenses. These studies have been and continue to be funded by the National Institute on Drug Abuse. I was already doing this research when crack cocaine was first "discovered" in New York, so in my role as a government employee doing research on drugs and violence I was regularly asked to provide information about drug-related violence to state government policy-makers.

The New York State office where I worked was a unit of the Division of Criminal Justice Services (DCJS), organizationally a division of the Executive Department. For most of the time I was there, our Commissioner was simultaneously the Governor's Director of Criminal Justice. So through the Director our job was to provide the Governor with information and recommendations for policy and program development. Our office, the Office of Justice Systems Analysis (OJSA), had three bureaus—policy, research, and statistics. Ideally, the statistics bureau managed the data bases and generated the official crime statistics for the State, the research bureau used that data to do policy-oriented research about crime and criminal justice, and the policy bureau used the statistics and research findings to conduct policy analyses and to draft policy and program initiatives. (It never really worked that smoothly, but that was the idea.)

In my last years at DCJS I was Chief of the Bureau of Statistical Services. In that role I was responsible for the collection of statewide crime and criminal justice data and for the construction and maintenance of the state's official crime and criminal justice data bases and statistics, including the Uniform Crime Reports.

When the crime index, particularly the violent crime index, began to decline in 1990, it was my office that gave the statistics, and hence the news, to the Governor's office. As the index of violent crime continued to decline, I was often asked by the State Director to provide an explanation for this dramatic turn of events. In a series of memoranda to the Director, I emphasized the significance of understanding the changing patterns of organization of the crack cocaine market for understanding both the rise of violence through the late 1980s and its subsequent decline in the early 1990s.

From my current position at a university in Maryland (where the violent crime rate is not falling), I am more an observer than a participant as the media and public officials try to explain the drop in violent crime now occurring throughout most of the nation. Criminologists point to demographics and drugs, and practitioners and policy-makers to their programs and policies. There is some truth to what they say, but contemporary explanations for the recent descent in the officially reported rates of violent crime in urban America are inadequate for two reasons. First, they focus primarily on the decline rather than on the overall context of change, including first the rise and then the fall. More important, they fail to acknowledge that the official indices of crime are in fact social constructions, and that the media, the government, and law enforcement play important roles in their construction. In this book, I demonstrate how these institutions first participated in the construction of an epidemic of violent crime around crack cocaine, and then used that epidemic to support an unprecedented expansion of the criminal justice system.

Social constructionism has a prominent place in contemporary social problems theory. Based on the writings of theorists such as Alfred Schutz, Peter Berger, and others, social constructionism argues that the problems of society are properly understood as the product of the decisions, interpretations, actions, and interactions of individuals engaged in a common social setting or context. The phenomenon or phenomena that we call crime, even violent crime, is thus the social product of the decisions, interpretations, actions, and interactions of individuals with varying degrees of power and authority, each making claims about what crime is and how much of it there is. Crime is culturally defined in that those making claims about it use symbols and styles of culture and subculture to support their claims, which would otherwise be unsubstantiated.

To understand social problems, constructionists naturally focus on social action and on claims and claims-makers in a social arena. Contextual constructionists study claims and claims-makers particularly in the context of a specific social setting or social conditions. This book provides a contextual constructionist analysis of the rise and fall of the official index of violent crime in the U.S. from 1980 to 1994, with special attention to the New York City experience. In it, I describe how the decisions, interpretations, actions, and interactions of criminal justice policy-makers and analysts, law enforcement officials and officers, and news reporters, all acting effectively as claims-makers in the context of an evolving crack cocaine market, contributed to the construction of the rise and fall of a violent crime wave.

Acknowledgments

This book reflects knowledge I have accumulated and ideas I have thought about over my years in government and academia. Like all social phenomena, knowledge and ideas are social constructions. What I know and what I think, therefore, is truly the product of my experience with other people around me. I would like to thank at least a few of those people who have contributed to this work.

Over dinner at the American Society of Criminology meeting in Boston in 1995, I spoke to Marty Schwartz and Dragan Milovanovic about my idea for this book. Not only did they share their thoughts and encourage me at that time, but over the years I have drawn extensively from my too few opportunities to spend time and talk with them. I also thank Dragan for directing me to Graeme Newman, and I thank Graeme for agreeing to publish this book through Harrow and Heston.

Once I started writing, I benefited from discussions with Arnie Sherman, Howard Gersh, and many others, including my colleagues at the University of Baltimore, especially Niki Benokraitis and Kathy Block. My students, often unbeknownst to them, acted as sounding boards for some of my ideas, and I thank them for that, particularly George Payer, who was my Graduate Assistant. George found whatever I asked him to find in the library, even if it was hidden somewhere deep in cyberspace.

For more than a decade at the New York State Division of Criminal Justice Services, I worked with so many people who not only listened to my ideas about government, policy, research, bureaucracy and just about anything else, but shared theirs with me. Those to whom I owe a debt for helping me to formulate some of the ideas in this book include Barry Sample, Chris Zimmerman, Vince Manti, Rich Hunter, Donna Hall, Jim Nelson, Dick Ely, and Therese Shady.

At National Development and Research Institutes, Inc., I have engaged in research with a succession of talented and stimulating people. For their contribution to my thinking about what is discussed in this book, I thank especially Susan Crimmins, Barry Spunt, and Paul Goldstein. I also owe a debt to Fred Streit, who created an environment at NDRI in which good research could be conducted, and gave me an opportunity to work in that environment despite my organizational ties to other agencies. I thank as well our project managers at the National Institute of Justice, Bud Gropper, and at the National Institute on Drug Abuse, Mario De La Rosa and Coryl Jones, who have continuously supported and continue to support the research I have been doing at NDRI.

Finally, I thank my wife Cindy and my daughters, Becky and Liz. They were patient and considerate the many days and nights I was "locked" in my office and not available to be with them. There is always the next consuming project, but hopefully now we can spend more time together.

In the end, opinions and points of view expressed herein are mine alone, and do not necessarily reflect nor represent those of any other individual, agency, or organization.

*I dedicate this work to the memory
of my father,
Maury Brownstein.*

1

The Wave of Violent Crime

On as crisp fall day in 1995, William Bratton, then Commissioner of the New York City Police Department, the NYPD, returned home to Boston to address an audience of criminologists gathered for the annual meeting of the American Society of Criminology. Commissioner Bratton was in the city of his youth, a city he had earlier served as the head of its police department. An estimated 200 criminologists were present to hear him explain why crime, most notably violent crime, had been falling so precipitously in New York City for almost five years.

With obvious pride, Bratton began by reading the latest statistics to his audience. As of that very morning, violent crime in New York City was continuing its downward slide. He offered a cavalier dismissal of other explanations for the decline, such as changes in the demographic characteristics of the city's populace, and concluded with a polemic on how police programs and practices had successfully reduced crime and violence in the city.

The Commissioner was followed on the podium by three prominent criminologists, each of whom responded to his remarks. With due respect, one argued for the significance of the changing nature of the crack trade as an explanation for the decline. Another supported Bratton's argument that police work had made the difference. The third kindly told the Commissioner that his conclusions were simplistic and that all he need do is ask and any number of the hundreds of criminologists present at the meeting would be happy to help him to understand the City's good fortune.

Throughout the plenary, all four speakers and the moderator remained focused on the decline of crime in the 1990s. In that sense, they were not placing the story in its proper context: the notable rise and *then* fall of violent crime in just over a decade. The story of the decline of violent crime in American communities is always and without doubt an interesting story. But in this case it is really the story of a crime wave, the apparent decrease having been preceded by an increase that was just as palpable. In any event, it can only be understood in terms of the social, cultural, and political context in which it occurred.

In this chapter official crime statistics are presented to demonstrate both the rise and fall of violent crime in the United States during the last two decades of the twentieth century. The next chapter will consider the statistics that are used as a measure of violent crime and the process through which they are constructed. Subsequent chapters will include discussions of the social, political, and cultural context of the crime wave, specifically in terms of the significance of crack cocaine and the claims-making roles of government policy-makers, law enforcement officials, and the news media in the social construction of the problem of violent crime.

Violence and Violent Crime

While violence may in simple terms be defined as the use of force to gain dominance over another or others, in its social realization it takes a variety of forms ranging "from political violence, through the violence of occupations, criminal violence, violence in the home, to the violence of those who are sick, and many other different forms" (Newman 1979, 5). The definition of violence is complicated further in that whatever form it takes, the classification of any behavior or action as violent is inevitably determined in a social and political—that is, ideological—context (Arendt 1969; Sorel 1950; Stigliano 1983). A behavior or action cannot be identified as violence by the nature of the behavior or action alone, but rather by its interpretation as violent.

Such is the case with what is commonly called *criminal violence*. For the official purpose of classifying crimes as violent for the Uniform Crime Reports (UCR), the federal government defines violent crime as "composed of four offenses: murder and nonnegligent manslaughter, forcible rape, robbery, and aggravated assault. All violent crimes involve force or threat of force" (Federal Bureau of Investigation 1994, 10). The states use the same definition for UCR purposes, but may have a different legal definition of violent crime. For example, New York State legally classifies certain crimes as "violent felony offenses" for purposes of prosecution and sentencing, and the crimes included in this legal category are not all the same offenses as those classified as violent for UCR purposes (Division of Criminal Justice Services 1995, 185). Offenses not considered violent under UCR definition, such as weapons offenses and other sex offenses, are considered violent felonies in New York.

Criminal violence may have an ideological basis, but UCR statistics are the official measure of violent crime in the U.S. Reports of violence by government and the media typically refer to the violent crimes counted for UCR purposes. In addition, when the public expresses concern about violence, that concern is more than likely expressed in terms of crimes included in the UCR index of violent crime (National Commission on the Causes and Prevention of Violence 1969; Weiner and Wolfgang 1985).

The Violent Crime Wave in the United States: 1980 to 1994

The wave of violent crime that was observed in the U.S. from the early 1980s to the middle of the 1990s was, according to official statistics, real. However, as impressive as it might have been, it was not really quite so exceptional. In trying to understand what was happening, Roth concluded, "Violence is a pervasive national problem, more serious in the United States than in the rest of the industrialized world, and especially serious for males who belong to demographic and ethnic minorities. However, the problem is neither unprecedented nor intractable" (1994b, 10).

Official records of crime across the nation were not collected and maintained in the United States until 1930, when the Federal Bureau of Investigation began the Uniform Crime Reports program. Given the usual difficulties of starting a national program and changes and improvements made over the first decades of operation, contemporary UCR index crime statistics are not really comparable to statistics maintained prior to 1958 (President's Commission 1968, 104). However, the Commission on Law Enforcement and Administration of Justice established in 1965 by President Lyndon Johnson "adjusted unpublished figures from the UCR" and examined crime index trends from 1933 to 1965 (President's Commission 1968, 104). They concluded the following:

> For crimes of violence the 1933-65 period . . . has been . . .
> one of sharply divergent trends for the different offenses.
> Total numbers for all reported offenses have increased

markedly; the Nation's population has increased also—by
more than 47 percent since 1940. The number of offenses per
100,000 population has tripled for forcible rape and has
doubled for aggravated assault during the period, both
increasing at a fairly constant pace. The willful homicide rate
has decreased somewhat to about 70 percent of its high in
1933, while robbery has fluctuated from a high in 1933 and a
low during World War II to a point where it is now about 20
percent above the beginning of the postwar era. The overall
rate for violent crimes, primarily due to the increased rate for
aggravated assault, now stands at its highest point, well
above what it has been throughout most of the period.
(President's Commission 1968, 104)

Generally, the rate of violent index crime declined from 1933
through the early 1940s, rose slightly after World War II, and
remained on a fairly level plane until around 1960, when it rose
sharply.

After 1965, when there were reported through the UCR to
have been nearly 200 violent crimes per 100,000 population, the
violent crime rate continued to rise steadily and rapidly. By 1972
the rate approached 400 violent crimes per 100,000 population,
and by 1980 it was almost 600.

According to UCR statistics, the really big increases in violent crime came during the 1960s, and to a lesser extent the 1970s
(Federal Bureau of Investigation 1993, 58-9). From 1960 to 1970,
the rate of violent index crime rose 126 percent (from 159.6 to
361.0 violent crimes per 100,000 population). From 1970 to 1980
the rate rose 65 percent (from 361.0 to 596.6 violent crimes per
100,000 population). From 1980 to 1990, the rate rose only 23
percent (from 596.6 to 731.8 violent crimes per 100,000 population). (See Table 1, below.)

Nonetheless, the UCR rates of violent crime from 1980 to
1994, years encompassing the introduction of crack cocaine and
the evolution of crack markets in U.S. cities, are currently captur-

ing the imagination of U.S. policy-makers, law enforcement officials, the news media, and the public. From 1980 to 1994, the
number of UCR violent crimes in the U.S. increased from 1.3
million to 1.9 million, or 39 percent (Federal Bureau of Investigation 1995, 58). During this period, the population of the U.S. grew
from 213 million to 260 million, so the rate of violent crime per
every 100,000 population increased by only 20 percent. Table 2,
below, shows the UCR rates for the total, violent, and property
crime indices, as well as rates for specific violent crimes, reported
through the Uniform Crime Reports program for the U.S. from
1980 to 1994.

Table 1
Percent Increase in UCR Violent Crime Rate, By Decade

Decade	Percent Change in Violent Crime Rate
1960-1970	126%
1970-1980	65%
1980-1990	23%

Source: Federal Bureau of Investigation, 1993, *Crime in the U.S., 1992* .

According to these UCR statistics, the violent crime rate
declined annually in the U.S. from 1980 through 1983, increased
almost continuously through 1991, and then began to decline
again. The increase from 1984 to 1991, 41 percent, was the most
dramatic of the period. The property crime rate also rose and fell
over this period, but the variation was not as impressive; from 1985
to 1991, the property crime rate increased by 14 percent. In terms
of specific violent crimes, the homicide rate did increase by 24
percent from 1984 to 1991, but was higher in 1980 than in any year
since. The robbery rate increased by 33 percent from 1984 to 1991,
but was lower in 1994 than in any of the first years of the 1980s.
Assault showed the greatest and most consistent increase among

Table 2

Selected U.S. UCR Crime Rates, 1980-1994

Source: Federal Bureau of Investigation, 1995, *Crime in the U.S., 1994*

YEAR	Total Index Crime Rate	Violent Crime Rate	Property Crime Rate	Murder and NonNeg Mansl'ter	Forcible Rape	Robbery	Agg. Assault
1980	5,950.0	596.6	5,353.3	10.2	36.8	251.1	298.5
1981	5,858.2	594.3	5,263.9	9.8	36.0	258.7	289.7
1982	5,603.6	571.1	5,032.5	9.1	34.0	238.9	289.2
1983	5,175.0	537.5	4,637.4	8.3	33.7	216.5	279.2
1984	5,031.3	539.2	4,492.1	7.9	35.7	205.4	290.2
1985	5,207.1	556.6	4,650.5	7.9	37.1	208.5	302.9
1986	5,480.4	617.7	4,862.6	8.6	37.9	225.1	346.1
1987	5,550.0	609.7	4,940.3	8.3	37.4	212.7	351.3
1988	5,664.2	637.2	5,027.1	8.4	37.6	220.9	370.2
1989	5,741.0	663.1	5,077.9	8.7	38.1	233.0	383.4
1990	5,820.3	731.8	5,088.5	9.4	41.2	257.0	424.1
1991	5,897.8	758.1	5,139.7	9.8	42.3	272.7	433.3
1992	5,660.2	757.5	4,902.7	9.3	42.8	263.6	441.8
1993	5,484.4	746.8	4,737.6	9.5	41.1	255.9	440.3
1994	5,374.4	716.0	4,658.3	9.0	39.2	237.7	430.2

the violent crime rates, increasing by 49 percent from 1984 to 1991 and remaining 44 percent higher in 1994 than it was in 1980. The official forcible rape rate did not change much over the period, increasing only 18 percent from 1984 to 1991.

Graphically, the pattern of the total violent crime rate in the U.S. from 1980 to 1984 took the form of a wave. (See Figure 1 .) It might not have had the drama of sea water, rising angrily in the ocean and then advancing thunderously to the shore. It might not have had the excitement of a progression of thousands of people standing and sitting in sequence with arms raised in ovation. And it certainly did not have the relative height of peaks achieved in earlier expansions of violent crime in the U.S. Nonetheless, from the early 1980s toward the end of the century, violent crime passed through the U.S. as a whole and through most major cities as a wave.

The Crime Wave as an Urban Phenomenon

The federal Panel on the Understanding and Control of Violent Behavior—established jointly by the National Science Foundation, the National Institute of Justice, and the Centers for Disease Control to render a broad appraisal of violence in the U.S.—recently concluded that violence "occurs most often in urban areas" (Roth 1994b, 2). However, the wave of violent crime that passed through the U.S. at the end of the century did not rise and fall equally in all cities. Table 3, below, compares the two largest cities to a medium size city and a smaller city and shows that the wave passed through earlier in the largest cities, but may have been more pronounced in the smaller cities.

In New York City, with a population of over 7 million people throughout the period, the rate of violent index crime peaked in 1990, 29 percent above its level in 1984. In Los Angeles, with a population that grew from almost 3 million to more than 3.5

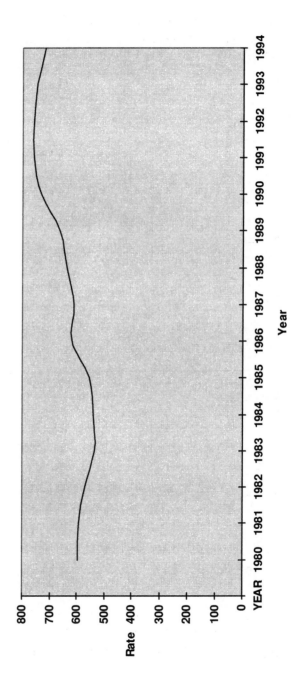

Figure 1
The Wave of Violent Crime: U.S., 1980-1984

Table 3

The Rate of Violent Crime in Selected Cities: 1980-1994

Year	New York City	Los Angeles	Baltimore, MD	Montgomery, AL
1980	2,125.7	1,742.5	2,112.2	520.8
1981	2,219.8	1,742.5	2,224,3	475.6
1982	2,028.3	1,739.4	2,090.1	372.1
1983	1,868.3	1,691.7	2,002.7	289.0
1984	1,845.8	1,636.1	1,975.8	238.5
1985	1,881.3	1,658.0	2,009.9	292.9
1986	1,995.2	2,035.6	1,943.6	210.2
1987	2,036.1	1,910.2	1,868.9	168.1
1988	2,217.6	1,961.5	1,927.1	234.5
1989	2,299.9	2,246.1	2,046.5	356.9
1990	2,383.6	2,404.6	2,437.7	516.8
1991	2,318.2	2,525.8	2,544.0	903.6
1992	2,163.7	2,459.5	2,885.3	775.4
1993	2,089.8	2,374.3	2,994.0	871.9
1994	1,860.9	2,059.0	2,834.5	964.3

Source: Federal Bureau of Investigation, *Crime in the U.S.*, 1980 to 1994

million during the period, the rate of violent index crime peaked in 1991, 54 percent above its 1984 level. In Baltimore, Maryland, with a population that declined from almost 800,000 to around 740,000 during the period, the rate of violent index crime was at its highest in 1993, 52 percent above its 1984 level, but may not yet have reached its peak for the current wave. In Montgomery, Alabama, with a population below 200,000 throughout the period, the rate of violent index crime was erratic and its variation extreme; it was at its highest in 1994, 300 percent greater than its 1984 level, and at its lowest in 1987, 474 percent below its 1994 level.

While increases in smaller cities may have been as large or larger than the increases in larger cities, the phenomenon of the

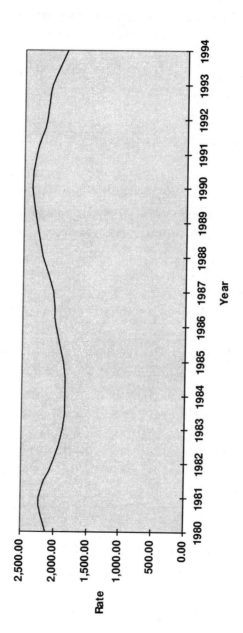

Figure 2
The Wave of Violent Crime: NYC., 1980-1994

contemporary violent crime wave is perhaps best demonstrated by the pattern of the violent crime rate in New York City. While the increase in New York may not have been the greatest among U.S. cities, the decline to date has been the most impressive. Figure 2, below, shows graphically the dramatic wave of violent crime that washed over New York City between 1980 and 1994.

Violent Crime and Violent Victimizations

As noted earlier, the Uniform Crime Reports are both the official record of crime in the United States and the primary measure of crime as it is defined by government policy-makers, law enforcement officials, the news media, and the public. Nonetheless, the UCR is not the only measure of criminal activity in the U.S. Since 1973, criminal victimizations have been counted under the direction of the Bureau of Justice Statistics through the National Crime Victimization Survey (NCS). The NCS is a survey of a sample of households and individuals age 12 or older in the U.S. (Bureau of Justice Statistics 1994). Personal crimes are distinguished from household crimes, the former comprising violent crimes for purposes of the survey. The personal crimes, actually victimizations, counted include female rape, robbery, and assault. While defined somewhat differently, these are comparable to three of the four crimes in the UCR violent crime index. For obvious reasons, homicide is not included in this survey of victims.

The considerable debate over the validity of the NCS as compared to the UCR, which will be discussed in the next chapter, suggests that each is a measure of something, though not necessarily the same thing. Nonetheless, it is interesting to look at the trend in violent victimizations over the period of the current UCR crime wave.

Because of changes in the NCS survey design, statistics collected since 1993 are "not directly comparable with data collected prior to 1993" (Perkins and Klaus 1996, 5). In addition, NCS statistics are only available on a national level. Still, given those limitations, NCS statistics indicate little fluctuation in the rate of violent victimizations from the year 1980 to 1992. (See Table 4, below.)

Table 4
Violent Victimizations in the U.S.: 1980-1992

Year	Violent Victimization Rate
1980	33.3
1981	35.3
1982	34.3
1983	31.0
1984	31.4
1985	30.0
1986	28.1
1987	29.3
1988	29.6
1989	29.8
1990	29.6
1991	32.2
1992	32.1

Source: Bureau of Justice Statistics, *Criminal Victimization in the U.S.: 1973-92 Trends*

The graphic demonstration of the extent to which there was a wave of violent crime in the U.S. by NCS accounting does not contain the drama of the UCR graphic account. From Figure 3, below, it is clear that by the standard of the NCS, there was not much of a wave of violent crime in the U.S. between 1980 and 1992. Perhaps the trend is better characterized as a trough, dropping slightly in the middle years, but not by much.

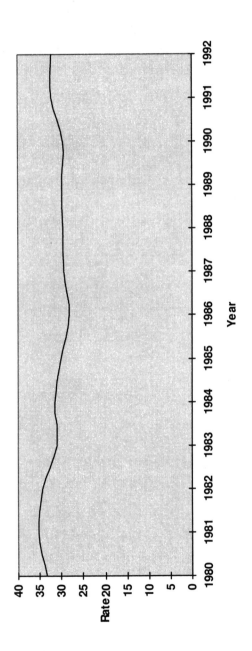

Figure 3

A Wave of Violent Victimizations? U.S., 1980-1992

Conclusion

On the surface, the violent crime index of the Uniform Crime Reports shows that a wave of violent crime did pass through the United States between 1980 and 1994. Looking deeper, it was not much of a wave, if it was one at all. First, the 23 percent increase in violent crime from 1980 to 1990 paled in comparison to the 126 percent increase from 1960 to 1970. Second, different violent index crimes followed different paths during this period, and except for aggravated assault, most of the variation in particular violent crime rates was fairly flat. Third, it was easy to see the pattern of violent crime as a wave in large urban centers, but not necessarily in other parts of the country. And finally, in terms of violent victimizations as measured by the NCS, the violent crime rate was more of a trough than a wave between 1980 and 1992.

In sum, the violent crime wave of the waning decades of the twentieth century was not particularly impressive. On the other hand, the response to it was most impressive. The question, then, is why during this period did violent crime get so much attention from government policy-makers, law enforcement officials, the news media, and the public? That question will be addressed in the chapters that follow.

2

The Measurement of Violent Crime

The nature and extent of violent crime in the United States is typically measured as part of the crime index of the Uniform Crime Reports (UCR), which represents the "official" estimate of crime in the nation. Though the index is commonly treated as an objective measure of crime, it is actually a social, cultural, and historical construction.

Official Crime Statistics

In general, official statistics are those "that governments produce, finance, or routinely incorporate into their decisions" (Starr 1987, 8, fn 1). They are generated from data provided by criminal justice administrators and law enforcement practitioners to localities, the states, and the federal government. These governments collect and tabulate these data and disseminate them in the form of reports, bulletins, memoranda, and so on. For more than two decades the reliability and validity of official crime statistics, particularly the UCR, has been the subject of considerable debate (see Blumstein, Cohen, and Rosenfeld 1991, 1992; Eck and Riccio 1979; Gove, Hughes, and Geerken 1985; Hindelang, Hirschi, and Weis 1979; Jensen and Karpos 1993; Maltz 1975; Menard 1991, 1992; Menard and Covey 1988; McDowall and Loftin 1992; O'Brien 1990, 1991, 1996; Skogan 1974; Thornberry and Farnworth 1982).

The UCR program, administered by the Federal Bureau of Investigation (FBI), is the primary and most visible source of official crime statistics in the U.S. today. UCR statistics provide counts of specified offenses against people, businesses, organizations, and government agencies and are derived from police records. The program was originally planned in 1927 for the purpose of developing "a national system of statistics that would overcome variations in the way crimes were defined in different parts of the country" (Bureau of Justice Statistics 1988, 11). More precisely, as Maltz reports, a principle motivation for actually starting the program in 1930 was the concern of the International Association of the Chiefs of Police with "the publicity about 'crime waves' generated by the press" (1977, 32).

Serious questions about the reliability and validity of UCR statistics as a measure of crime arose when the National Crime Victimization Survey (NCS) was started in 1973. The purpose of that program is "to learn more about crimes and the victims of crime, ... to measure crimes not reported to police as well as those that are reported" (Bureau of Justice Statistics 1988, 11). Administered by the federal Bureau of Justice Statistics, NCS is a victimization survey that includes data on both reported and not reported offenses. It counts only crimes against a sample of persons 12 years of age and older and their households.

Invariably there is a discrepancy between the number and type of crimes reported by the official police statistics of UCR and the self-reported statistics of NCS. This inconsistency has led to the conclusion that many crimes go unreported to the police. These unreported crimes, the so-called "dark figure of crime," are considered to be an important source of UCR invalidity.

Naturally, crime researchers have tried to explain the discrepancy. Some have suggested that the difference between the two measures of crime could be explained by the fact that the official statistics of UCR and the self-reported statistics of NCS are derived from "different domains of criminal conduct" (Hindelang, Hirschi, and Weis, 1979; Thornberry and Farnworth 1982). From this perspective, both measure something about crime, though not necessarily the same thing.

Gove, Hughes, and Geerken argued that "the UCR appear to reflect fairly accurately what the citizens and police perceive as violations of the law which pose a significant threat to the social order" (1985, 490). Thinking of citizens and the police as "filters" through which selected events are officially labeled as crime, they wrote, "it is important to note that if one defines crime as criminal acts serious enough to be reacted to by both citizens and the police, then from the evidence reviewed above, the UCR are at least as valid and probably more valid than the data from victimization surveys" (1985, 491).

Arguing that "Gove et al. were unduly optimistic about the validity of UCR," Menard and Covey used UCR and NCS data across time and location to show that UCR and NCS statistics give attention to different types and levels of crime (1988, 381). This approach moved the debate to comparisons of UCR and NCS statistics in terms of the strength of the relationship of the two time series (see Blumstein, Cohen, and Rosenfeld 1991, 1992; Menard 1991, 1992; O'Brien 1990, 1991). Blumstein and his associates argued that there is "some important consistency between UCR and NCS crime data over time" (1991, 257) and Menard countered that "the series are best regarded as indicators of two separate and distinct phenomena" (1992, 105). Accepting both as measures of something about crime, McDowall and Loftin tried to shift the direction of this discourse with the suggestion that a "more useful strategy might be to assume that both measures contain significant errors and that both can be improved if the errors are discovered" (1992, 131).

Even before NCS was established, the rationale for a crime statistics debate could be found in an article written more than three decades ago by Kitsuse and Cicourel (1963). They argued then that official crime statistics, UCR, reflect "specifically organizational contingencies which condition the application of specific statutes to actual conduct through the interpretations, decisions, and actions of law enforcement personnel" (1963, 137). The simplistic response to that conclusion is that UCR statistics are invalid, and the article was widely cited as evidence of that invalidity.

While it is possible to argue from the Kitsuse and Cicourel article that UCR statistics are not a valid measure of crime, that is not the point the authors were making. Rather than suggesting that official statistics of crime should be rejected as invalid, they wrote, "we have taken the view that official statistics, reflecting as they do the variety of organizational contingencies in the process by which deviants are differentiated from non-deviants, are sociologically relevant data" (1963, 139). That is, to be worthwhile, the discourse about official crime statistics should be about the constructed nature of the various measures of crime.

The Construction of UCR Statistics

For more than two years as Chief of the Bureau of Statistical Services for the New York State Division of Criminal Justice Services (DCJS), I was responsible for the collection, maintenance, and dissemination of official crime and criminal justice data and statistics in New York State. I managed a staff of 25 people who designed, developed, and operated a variety of statewide data bases and statistical reporting programs, including the UCR and its projected successor the Incident-Based Reporting program, an offender-based transaction statistics program called the Trends file, a prosecution-based program called the Indictment Statistical System, the Bias Crime Reporting program, the Automated Criminal Justice Indicator System, and others.

Under the New York State Executive Law sections 837 and 837-a, DCJS is granted broad authority and obligation to collect, analyze, and disseminate criminal justice data. Under section 837-b, all statewide courts and peace officers are required to report this information routinely. The agency has combined this responsibility with its voluntary commitment to provide relevant data to the national UCR program (DCJS 1995, iv).

The UCR data are submitted monthly by law enforcement agencies around the State. They include information about the extent of specified violent and property crimes that are considered serious, the number of other lesser crimes, the value of property stolen, the location and time of offenses, the number of arrests for both serious and lesser crimes, the number of law enforcement officers killed or assaulted, and the number of law enforcement employees in the State (DCJS 1995).

Through its production of a *Crime and Justice Annual Report*, similar to the FBI's UCR report, *Crime in the U.S.*, DCJS constructs an official definition or picture of the current crime problem for the State of New York. Official DCJS statistical reports, including the *Crime and Justice Annual Report* as well as several specialized bulletins and memoranda published throughout the year, rarely provide an analysis or interpretation of the numbers presented. Rather, they are depicted as an objective presentation of facts that others may use first to draw conclusions and then to make policy or take action. In fact, the statistics are simply tabulations and calculations derived from the raw data reported by law enforcement officials to the State. That is, using UCR statistics, government-based claims are made about how much crime there is, where it is, who is responsible for it, and even about what is and what is not crime.

Under federal UCR guidelines, crimes are separated as Part I and Part II offenses. The seven Part I offenses, which form the crime index, are deemed "serious." These include: homicide, forcible rape, robbery, aggravated assault, burglary, larceny, and motor vehicle theft. (An attempt to add arson to the index was not successful; at this time it is not included at all in New York and is included only in a "modified index" at the federal level.) For these offenses, data collected include information about both the number of offenses known to the police and the number of arrests made. Part II offenses, which are considered less serious and about which less information is collected, include more than 25 offenses from kidnapping through fraud and embezzlement to public intoxication and loitering. All drug offenses are Part II offenses, a decision that might have been made differently had the crime index been created in the 1980s.

The New York Experience. Theoretically, UCR data are voluntarily submitted monthly to DCJS from more than 600 local law enforcement agencies. A staff of four data entry clerks, a supervisor, and an administrator receive around 800 completed forms each month. All UCR data are received on forms completed by hand. The data on these forms are verified by a senior clerk and entered into the agency computer by a data entry clerk. While staff work hard and try to maintain high data quality standards, even at this early stage in the construction of UCR statistics it is clear that these numbers are the product of what Kitsuse and Cicourel referred to as "interpretations, decisions, and actions" (1963).

First, budget cutbacks in recent years forced an elimination of field staff who trained and assisted UCR clerks in local police agencies. Consequently, local law enforcement agency staff who prepare the forms to submit to the State are not trained, and can only get answers to questions about the forms and procedures for completing them from a handbook that had not been revised in almost two decades (DCJS 1977) or over the telephone. The high turnover rate among the UCR clerks in local agencies exacerbates this problem. The people completing the forms, therefore, have to decide what to enter and how to enter it without having adequate training or support.

The mainframe computer programs that are used by DCJS for the UCR program were written so long ago that frequently programmers at the agency who work on these programs cannot find the original source code, so have no way of knowing what the programs are actually doing. To complicate this problem, many of these programs are cumbersome and inefficient, doing things the way they were done before the advent of personal computers and computer networks.

Four poorly paid clerks doing the tedious work of data entry with little or no possibility of overtime, which is discouraged because of budgetary constraints, often maintain a monthly backlog of as many 1,000 submitted forms to enter. As FBI deadlines approach, such as the April deadline to submit statistics for major cities and the summer deadline to submit all statistics for the previous year, the clerks and their supervisor scurry to enter as much as possible. Even diligent and hardworking people have difficulty maintaining their usual standard of quality control under these circumstances.

As a result of local politics, decisions and assumptions must be made by data entry personnel about how to count and enter the data received. This is apparent in what is called the "New York City reconciliation." As localities and agencies within localities compete amongst themselves for a greater share of State resources, they all compete to show that they are responsible for a greater share of the problem that the resources will be used to solve. Consequently, everyone wants credit for reported crimes and arrests. In New York City, where there are so many competing jurisdictions and agencies, this translates as a problem of duplicate reporting. So every summer a senior data entry clerk conducts the reconciliation, separating out by hand and by assumption the duplicate reports of the same crimes and arrests submitted by different jurisdictions and agencies.

Given deadlines that are set so statistics can be reported in a timely fashion for policy-making and law enforcement purposes, decisions must be made that impact on what will be reported as crime. Every spring, for example, the FBI publishes its index of crime statistics for major cities in the U.S. for the previous year. To do so, the FBI needs to receive these statistics from the states by a particular date. It is possible that the designated major cities in a state have not submitted all their forms for the previous year by that date. In New York, data entry staff call and cajole their counterparts in those cities, getting what they can, even rough estimates if necessary, to meet the deadline. New York City, of course, has submitted nothing by that date so annually holds up the State submission to the FBI until the City releases its own statistics to the media, after which time those numbers are sent to the State to forward to the FBI for the major cities report.

Deadlines are also significant to the construction of official crime statistics in that the federal and state deadlines are not the same. Localities can submit forms to the State for the previous year as late as July or even August of the following year, and later if the State would allow it. However, States must report UCR statistics to the FBI in time for the FBI to prepare and release *Crime in the U.S.* In past years that report was released in August for the previous year, more recently it has not been released until the fall but before the end of the current year. To meet the FBI deadline,

New York would send the FBI what it had as close to the FBI deadline as possible, depending on when the New York City reconciliation could be completed. If a locality had not submitted all of its forms from the previous year by that date, usually early-summer, it would not be included in what was sent to the FBI. The State releases its own annual report after the federal report is released, so it continues to receive and enter data from the local-ities beyond the FBI closing date. Consequently, the New York State crime statistics in the FBI's *Crime in the U.S.* do not match the New York State crime statistics in the State's *Crime and Justice Annual Report.*

Incident-Based Reporting. UCR statistics are aggregate sta-tistics. That is, they are submitted, entered, and reported as counts of crime and arrest. No detail is provided about specific events that are included in those counts. It is not possible to know what "interpretations, decisions, and actions" went into the aggregation of the data. This tends to mask the constructed nature of the statistics. Over the years there have been two UCR programs designed to collect incident-based crime data. To date, neither has been very successful, but both provide some insight into the process by which crime statistics are constructed.

The Supplementary Homicide Reports (SHR) collects data on individual homicide events reported under the UCR program. For SHR, data are collected each month on forms that are voluntarily submitted by all police jurisdictions in the U.S. to the states for the FBI. For each case of murder or non-negligent manslaughter that occurs within a local jurisdiction in New York, for example, information is provided "regarding the homicide victim, offender, their relationship, the weapon used, and circumstances" of the cases (DCJS 1977, 66).

Under the SHR reporting format, to report the circumstance of a particular homicide, the person filling out the form is given a space 3/8 inch by 3½ inches and instructed to "furnish a brief statement as to the victim's death" (DCJS 1977, 69). While they are encouraged to use as much of the space as necessary to describe the event, they are directed to provide details about only one attribute of the event. Highest priority is given to its relationship, should there be one, to any other crime.

Given this system, the SHR program naturally underreports certain types of homicide. For example, the robbery of a drug dealer resulting in his or her death could be entered on the form simply as a "robbery killing." However, the person completing the form is free to write "drug-related robbery killing." There is no way of knowing what decisions are being made in the classification of homicide circumstances, but it is clear that decisions are being made that have an impact on how the nature of homicide is measured.

In recent years the FBI has been supporting the development of a new UCR program. There have been efforts in some states to develop an operational Incident-Based Reporting (IBR) system, that would change the UCR from aggregated to case level data collection. Under a fully operational IBR program, data on crimes known to the police would be collected nationwide from the various states and maintained by the FBI. In addition to case identifiers and a notation of incident status, data would be collected on the offense, the victim, property involved, the offender, and on the arrestee. In addition, IBR data would include information about the witnesses and a narrative describing the incident. After years of development, implementation is slow at best because of limited support for the program, but also because the federal, state, and local governments cannot reach agreement about how the program should operate. For example, many local agencies are still asking what value the program will have for their operation and at what cost.

Changes in Policy and Practice. The constructed nature of crime statistics is also made apparent by changes in crime or criminal justice policy or practice, even on the local level. An example from New York City demonstrates how a local decision about how to count crimes can impact dramatically on the definition of a crime problem.

In New York City in 1980 there were 14,339 drug sales offenses reported in the UCR. In 1981 there were only 4,317. The difference is remarkable. Could the number of drug sales really have dropped so sharply in one year? When I first inquired in the early 1990s of the people who prepared the *Crime and Justice Annual Report* for those years, I was told that it must be a misprint. But the number for 1979 was 14,007 (close to the 1980 number) and for 1982 it was 3,950 (close to the 1981 number), so that explanation was not plausible.

No one who worked on the New York State UCR program during those years could explain with certainty what had happened more than a decade earlier. An administrator of the UCR unit did remember two informal, unwritten policy shifts around that time that redefined how drug sales offenses were counted in New York City. First, given how long it took them to get to the scene of a reported drug sale as compared to how quickly drug dealers could leave the scene, the police began to count as crimes only the drug sales they actually observed. Telephone complaints from citizens were no longer counted as crimes known to the police. Second, rather than counting each arrest of a drug dealer as a single crime, police began counting each drug sales scene as one crime, no matter how many people were arrested for drug sales at that scene. Whether or not these unofficial and unstated policy decisions do in fact explain the sharp decrease in the official number of drug sales, and whether or not they are accurate recollections of what actually happened, they do demonstrate how purportedly objective official statistics are very easily modified by the assumptions and decisions of the individuals who construct them.

The Power of Official Crime Statistics

While it is clear that official crime statistics are a social construction, they continue to be viewed and treated as an objective reality for program and policy purposes, and that claim to objectivity for those purposes is problematic (Brownstein 1991a, 1995). Generally, statistics are used to make claims about crime and crime problems in that "[n]umbers, rates, and percentages help describe a problem's dimensions; they [give] a sense of the claim's urgency" (Best 1990, 45). Given their government sponsorship, official statistics though not necessarily more or less valid than other statistics are "one of the most common ways" that knowledge about social conditions is incorporated into the rhetoric of claims-makers (Best 1989, 284; see, also, Jenkins 1994a, 1994b).

In terms of crime and deviance, Kitsuse and Cicourel looked at 'bureaucratically organized agencies [that] are increasingly invested with social control functions" and noted that "statistics routinely used by these agencies are social facts par excellence" (1963, 139). That is, the association of these statistics with powerful government agencies tends to give them an aura of credibility and objectivity that makes them difficult to ignore (compare Best 1990, 61-62).

Power as defined by Weber refers to "the probability that one actor within a social relationship will be in a position to carry out his [or her] own will despite resistance" (Weber 1947, 152). In terms of the process of claims-making, this means that claims-makers with more power are more likely to have their claims accepted by others as real (compare Spector and Kitsuse 1974, 149 and 1987, 144). Yet power is merely a probability, so it is precarious and its authority must be legitimated in order to become durable. Whatever the reasons that people accept a particular system of authority as legitimate, "What is important is the fact that in a given case the particular claim to legitimacy is to a significant degree and according to its type treated as 'valid'" (Weber 1947, 327).

In contemporary U.S. society, government is granted power and authority primarily through law, which gives validity to its claim to legitimacy. So claims made by government, including official statistics, do enter the arena of claims-making from a position of power. That is, as representations of government, they have the advantages of high visibility, social legitimacy, and an imputed objectivity (compare Starr 1987).

The power of official statistics is particularly strong in the area of crime and criminal justice. By law, itself a social construction, the government dominates the observation and regulation of these areas of social activity. Referring to this problem for social scientists who study crime, Quinney and Wildeman wrote, "Most of the available statistics that criminologists have relied upon in their research and generalizations have been derived from official sources, that is from statistics gathered by agencies of government" (1977, 98).

Claims made and supported by powerful groups, such as the government, come to dominate public perception, to become taken-for-granted as real (compare Best 1990). Hence, they serve as the basis for future action both by citizens who believe the claims to be real and by policy-makers who build policy around them.

Such was the case with the crime statistics that demonstrated the wave of violent crime that passed through American communities between the middle of the 1980s and the middle of the 1990s. The official UCR violent crime index provided support for the notion of first an increase and then a decline in the level of violent crime in the U.S. But knowing that those statistics are in fact a social construction suggests that what really happened may not be so simple, and it was not.

In the following chapters I will discuss the role of various claims-makers in the social production and construction of the wave of violent crime. First I will look at how violence was produced in the context of emerging crack cocaine markets. Then I will look at the claims of government, law enforcement, and the media and consider how those claims-makers influenced and used the measurement and reality of violent crime to support their own interests.

Chapter 3

Crack Cocaine and Violent Crime

The crest of the violent crime wave came to the United States at the end of the 1980s. It flooded first over the largest city on each coast, New York and Los Angeles, and then trickled down over smaller cities and towns, following the progression of crack cocaine markets through inner city neighborhoods.

Much research conducted in the U.S. during that period of history clearly showed that the emergence of crack cocaine markets was somehow related to the wave of violent crime in more than a temporal fashion. Arguably, there was more criminal violence then in American communities. Certainly, a new chemical substance was being manufactured, distributed, and used illegally on the streets of American cities. However, the accumulation of knowledge about the crack/violence relationship proceeded more slowly than did the demand for information by criminal justice policy-makers and law enforcement practitioners. So instead of understanding the nature and extent of the problem and responding to it appropriately, policy-makers and practitioners constructed a problem that suited their needs and served their purposes. The spread of crack cocaine markets and the increase in the number of reported violent crimes in the U.S. were observable and measurable phenomena. The *epidemic* of crack cocaine and *crisis* of violent crime that accompanied it were social constructions.

The Social Construction Crime Problems

Social thought emerging from the nineteenth century left us with a paradox of social existence (Berger 1963, 129). For Max Weber, the locus of social reality is to be found in *social action*, which he defined as inclusive of "all human behaviour when and in so far as the acting individual attaches subjective meaning to it" (1947, 88). For Emile Durkheim, the basic unit of social reality is the *social fact*, which he defined as "every way of acting, fixed or not, capable of exercising on the individual an external constraint" (1938, 13). From the perspective of the sociology of knowledge, Berger and Luckmann suggest that this "dual character of society in terms of objective facticity *and* subjective meaning" presents us not with a paradox but rather with the proper question for the analysis of social reality: "How is it possible that subjective meanings *become* objective facticities?" (1966, 17).

Subjective meanings become objective facticities through the action and interaction of individuals. These meanings are typified and hence take form through the patterns of behavior of the individuals who participate in the action, and from others who have a stake in the social definition of that action. Social problems theorists have been most interested in the processes through which claims are made about the problems of social reality.

There is an ongoing debate among contemporary social theorists who otherwise are in agreement that the problems of society are most appropriately understood as social constructions (see Best 1989, 1993; Hazelrigg 1985; Miller and Holstein 1993; Pfohl 1985; Pollner 1993; Rafter 1992a, 1992b, 1990; Schneider 1985; Troyer 1992; Woolgar and Pawluch 1985a, 1985b). By distinguishing *strict* constructionism from *contextual* constructionism, Joel Best tried to mediate this debate (1989).

The essence of strict constructionism may be found in the assertion by Alfred Schutz that "Strictly speaking, there are no such things as facts, pure and simple" (1962, 5). Strict constructionists base their work on the phenomenology of Schutz (1962) and the social problems theory of Spector and Kitsuse (1987, 1974). They "focus on claims-making; they do not presume to judge the accuracy of the members' claims" (Best 1989, 246). However, it has been argued that strict constructionist analyses "seem unable to avoid the claim for the existence and/or constancy of at least one relevant condition" (Woolgar and Pawluch 1985a, 218). At the very least, and in spite of the effort to avoid objectivism, it is hard to think about any process without thinking about its context.

Contextual constructionists "remain focused on the claims-making process" but use "social conditions [or] refer to social conditions in explaining why some claims receive attention or shape social policy" (Best 1989, 247). Their interest lies both in the social realms within which *and* the processes by which claims-makers compete and collaborate to define or give meaning to the same social phenomenon or problem.

Generally, then, for contextual constructionists the efforts of claims-makers represent a competition or collaboration to define social reality. The objective of claims-making is to construct and confront others with a particular image of some social phenomenon. To do so, the claimant presents the image as if it were what Durkheim called a *social fact*. That is, the task of claims-making is to objectify reality, to generate through human activity "products . . . that are available both to their producers and to other men as elements of a common world" (Berger and Luckmann 1966, 33). Once a claim has been objectified, it assumes the quality of an objective facticity, "It is there, something that cannot be denied and that must be reckoned with" (Berger and Luckmann 1966, 91). It was through this process that the *crisis* of crack-related violence became a reality.

The Social Origins of the Crack Market in the U.S.

Several hundred years passed between the first written account of the use of coca leaves for getting high and the manufacture of crack cocaine for widespread distribution (see Inciardi 1992, 105). Nonetheless, crack cocaine did not suddenly appear on the streets of U.S. cities, and the time and location of its emergence and spread was not without reason. Crack does not appear in nature; it had to be produced by people.

Several things happened in the 1970s and 1980s in the U.S. that ultimately resulted in the introduction of crack to American drug users. First, the cultivation of coca leaves, the source of cocaine, expanded dramatically in the three Andean countries that are the greatest source of U.S. cocaine: Peru, Bolivia, and Colombia. According to government reports, between 1985 and 1988, coca leaf production grew by almost two-thirds in these three countries (Office of National Drug Control Policy 1989, 62). With the increased supply of coca leaf, the price of manufactured cocaine dropped and the purity of available cocaine increased. According to a report from the U.S. Attorney General's Office to the President, "Between 1982 and 1988, the wholesale price of a kilo of cocaine fell from a national range of $47,000 to $70,000 to a range of approximately $11,000 to $34,000. In the past 15 years, average purity rates for cocaine have risen over 300 percent, from a range of 10 to 20 percent purity to approximately 70 percent" (Office of the Attorney General 1989, 7). The result was more and higher quality cocaine on the streets.

Given the increased quantity and quality of cocaine, the need for an expanded market of users was apparent. Traditionally, cocaine has been distributed to users in the form of cocaine hydrochloride, processed largely in Colombia from coca leaves. In the U.S. in the 1960s, use of this powder moved to the mainstream culture, where it was typically sniffed or snorted for social or recreational purposes (Inciardi 1992, 108). Its use and consequently its market was limited by its cost. This market could not support the abundance of cocaine available in the 1970s and 80s.

One method of using cocaine that grew in popularity in the 1970s was freebasing. Inciardi and his colleagues describe freebase as follows:

> Freebase cocaine is a different chemical product from
> cocaine itself. In the process of preparing freebase, street
> cocaine—which is usually in the form of a hydrochloride
> salt—is treated with a liquid base (such as buffered
> ammonia) to remove the hydrochloric acid. The free cocaine
> (cocaine in the *base* state, *free* of the hydrochloric acid, and
> hence the name 'freebase') is then dissolved in a solvent such
> as ether, from which the purified cocaine is crystallized.
> These crystals, having a lower melting point, are then
> crushed and smoked in a special heated glass pipe. (Inciardi,
> Lockwood, and Pottieger 1993, p. 4)

By the late 1970s, perhaps 10 percent of the estimated 4,000,000 cocaine users in the U.S. were freebasers, seeking the "quicker and more potent" surge of euphoria (Inciardi 1992, 108-9).

Freebase proved to be complicated to make and dangerous to use (Inciardi 1992; Witkin 1991). Perhaps more relevant to the matter of finding a new market for cocaine products, however, freebase was not a less expensive alternative to cocaine powder. Whereas one gram of cocaine powder costing a user from $40 to

$120 could last a full weekend, "with freebasing, the cost factor can undergo a geometric increase" (Inciardi 1992, 109).

What freebase did do for cocaine was to demonstrate the existence of a market for a "simple form of smokable cocaine" that would offer a quick and intense rush of pleasure (Williams 1989, 1992; Witkin 1991). Crack would prove to be the perfect product for that market. Freebase is the cocaine product in its base state free of impurities. Crack is the cocaine product in its base state with impurities present. Specifically, crack is made by boiling in water equal amounts of cocaine hydrochloride and "comeback" (a cocaine analog, such as novocaine, as an additive) with half that amount of baking soda. When the boiling mixture forms a mass, put that in ice water until it hardens. When it is hard and dry, break it into pieces. In this way, just four ounces of cocaine hydrochloride "[s]erves 1,000" (Inciardi 1992, 116).

During the time when freebase was gaining popularity, crack was available on a small scale, but was considered an inferior product, sometimes referred to as "garbage freebase" (Inciardi 1992, 111). When the demand for a "simple form of smokable cocaine" became apparent, crack found its place. Crack as a product was easy to manufacture and handle, it could be sold in inexpensive quantities, and it had a reputation for providing a quick and pleasurable high (Bourgois 1995; Inciardi, Lockwood, and Pottieger 1993; Johnson, Hamid, and Sanabria 1992; Williams 1992). Crack markets had a high profit margin and the potential for high volume sales (Belenko 1990; Falco 1989; Inciardi 1989, 1992; Massing 1989; Office of the Attorney General 1989; Reuter, MacCoun, and Murphy 1990).

The remarkable popularity of crack, however, was actually a product of clever marketing. Crack was "invented" to provide a market for the oversupply of high quality and expensive cocaine hydrochloride available during the 1980s. As one news magazine reported, "What turned crack into a craze was mass marketing that

would have made McDonald's proud," (Witkin 1991, 44). As
Williams observed in his ethnographic study of crack in New York:

> Crack offered a chance to expand sales in ways never before
> possible because it was packaged in small quantities that sold
> for as little as two to five dollars. This allowed dealers to
> attract a new class of consumer: the persistent poor. Crack
> was sold on street corners, bringing the drug to people who
> could not pay the entrance fees to afterhours clubs or who
> would have been uncomfortable with the free-spending
> ambience in those places. In a very short time, crack was
> readily available in most poor neighborhoods. (Williams
> 1992, 9)

If cocaine were a legal product, the story of crack cocaine
would probably rival the story of microcomputers for the pages of
business newspapers and magazines.

Crack Markets and Violent Crime

Johnson, Hamid, and Sanabria distinguished two "ideal type"
drug markets (1992). The "business model" refers to those markets
that approximate "an organized profit-making enterprise ('business') with clear-cut employer-employee relationships" (1992,
62). According to Johnson and his associates:

> In this model, a higher level distributor ('dealer' or
> 'supplier') sets the terms of employment, provides ('fronts')
> [drug] supplies, and collects money regularly. While
> personnel turnover may be frequent, employees who have
> performed adequately can anticipate future drug supplies and
> expect a range of benefits such as bonuses, food, lodging,
> bail money, and so forth. (1992, 62)

Whatever form this model might approximate in the real
world, the maintenance of an ongoing, profit-making business
suggests the need for capital to acquire the product being marketed
and the resources to hire workers to market it on the street. The sale

of drugs is thus organized as a business, with interests specifically linked to profit-making and with relationships between employers and employees clearly delineated and routinized. Given these organizational and capital requirements, people are likely to enter the drug business as employees whose interests are defined in terms of wages and other forms of remuneration.

The other "ideal type" drug market model suggested by Johnson and his colleagues is the "free-lance model" in which "actors at all levels work together without clear employee-employer relationships being established" (Johnson, Hamid, and Sanabria 1992, 60). Under this model:

> All parties develop terms of agreement (how much money or drugs) for particular transactions. . . . Over several months, therefore, an individual will have many different partners. Dealers will provide supplies of [the drug] to several different sellers. Free-lance dealers may operate on either a 'cash' or 'consignment' basis. 'Cash only' dealers operate like most stores; the buyer must pay for the goods at point of purchase. Dealers who provide drugs on consignment (a loan or advance of [drugs]) expect the seller to return cash of about 50-70 percent of the value of the drugs at a specified future time. (Johnson, Hamid, and Sanabria 1992, 60)

In practice, the "free-lance model" in its various forms is likely to be found in open and unregulated economies where entrepreneurs with a small amount of product can establish themselves as drug dealers.

For several reasons, the first crack markets in the U.S. were established as "free-lance" markets. Only a few grams of cocaine were needed to produce enough crack for sale, so a limited capital investment was all that was required for anyone to become a crack distributor. In addition, crack was easy to manufacture through a process that could be accomplished at home. Because a small amount of crack resulted in an intense but brief high, the drug "lends itself to independent sales because customers make more frequent purchases of smaller amounts than they do with other drugs" (Inciardi, Lockwood, and Pottieger 1993). Finally, since crack was a new commodity, there were no established crack business hierarchies through which to manufacture and distribute the product. Consequently, the earliest crack markets were dominated by young, inexperienced individuals who started manufacturing and sales operations with as little as one or two grams of cocaine powder. As described in one news magazine at the time:

> The market in 1985 and early 1986 was still in its formative stages, however—marked not by massive organizations but by hundreds of cash-hungry young entrepreneurs. They worked out of apartments, using kitchen utensils. 'Anyone could buy the cocaine and make crack,' says the [New York City's] special narcotics prosecutor, Sterling Johnson. 'Back then, there was no General Motors of crack, just a lot of mom and pop operations.' (Witkin 1991, 49-50)

In theory at least, the early crack markets provided opportunities for ownership, control, and autonomy to anyone who could afford to purchase even a minimal amount of cocaine.

Violence is most likely to be used in a drug market economy by people who have an interest or stake in the drug trade and a willingness and ability to use violent means to protect or preserve their own interest or to acquire the interest of someone else. In an economy of independent entrepreneurs, those interests are dispersed and competition can be fierce. Consequently, the early "free-lance" crack markets tended to be more violent than other drug markets (Belenko 1990; Brownstein et al. 1992; Fagan and Chin 1990; Goldstein, Brownstein, and Ryan 1992; Goldstein et al. 1989; Mieczkowski 1990; Office of the Attorney General 1990). In addition, violence is more likely to be lethal when guns are involved, and crack markets emerged at the same time that semiautomatic handguns were becoming more widely available on the streets (Blumstein 1995; Roth 1994a; Shapiro 1996).

Young and heavily armed crack market entrepreneurs with little or no connection to established drug trafficking hierarchies operated independently and in conflict with one another to settle disputes over money and territory (Blumstein 1995). A study of homicides in New York City in 1988 found that more than half of all homicides were drug-related, about three-fourths of those were related to drug trafficking, and about two-thirds of those were related to crack (Brownstein et al. 1992; Goldstein, Brownstein, and Ryan 1992; Goldstein et al. 1989). Specifically, these cases involved disputes between dealers over territorial claims, disputes over the quality of drugs bought or sold, disputes over drug-related debt, and robberies of drug dealers.

During the years that the "free-lance" crack markets emerged and evolved, the level of reported violent crime continued to rise. For example, in New York City, one of the first cities in the U.S. to experience the establishment of a crack market, the official homicide rate rose from 19.3 killings per 100,000 population in 1985 to 30.7 in 1990, an increase of 59 percent (Division of Criminal Justice Services 1995, 8). Then, without warning, it began to fall. The homicide rate in New York City had dropped to 21.3 in 1994, a decline of 31 percent since its peak in 1990 and close to the level it was at when crack was first introduced.

Observers of the early crack market in New York City watched the level of violent crime change along with changes in the nature of the market itself (Johnson, Hamid, Sanabria 1992; Smith et al. 1992). Over time, free-lance crack dealers formed "confederations" through which they could continue to work independently while agreeing with other dealers to respect territory and not to compete for customers (Johnson, Hamid, and Sanabria 1992). As the market became increasingly organized, it eventually came to resemble what Johnson and his associates had called the "business model." That is, the manufacture and sale of crack was being organized on hierarchically and socially-controlled relationships between employers, employees, and customers.

As the crack market shifted from the free-lance to the business model, the organization, centralization, and hence stabilization of the crack trade followed the normal course of any emerging product market. In addition, the more that was learned about crack, the less exotic is became and the less ominous seemed its threat.

The Construction of a Crisis of Crack-Related Violence

Crack cocaine was invented and crack markets established to provide an outlet for the oversupply of cocaine that flooded the U.S. drug market in the 1970s and 1980s. At first the markets were dominated by young and independent entrepreneurs who operated independently of the social controls of established drug trafficking organizations and the law. These well-armed youngsters turned to violence to resolve disputes over such things as market share and product quality. Over time, the market evolved from the disorganized and extremely violent trade of autonomous young entrepreneurs, to confederations of independent dealers, to a more highly structured and less violent business-like industry.

The story of the evolution of crack markets and its relationship to violent crime has been well-documented by policy-oriented researchers and journalists. Beyond that, the greatest attention to crack and the crack trade has been given to the hysteria created about crack-related violence (Brownstein 1991a; Inciardi 1992; Johnson, Golub, and Fagan 1995; Reinarman and Levine 1989). For example, Reinarman and Levine have demonstrated how the *crisis* of crack-related violence was the construction of the news media and politicians working together in a conservative political context (1989). In the conclusion of their analysis they wrote, "In the current scare, the media's desire for dramatic drug stories interacted with politician's desire for safe election-year issues so that the news about crack spread to every nook and cranny of the nation far faster than dealers might have spread word on the street" (1989, 568).

Johnson, Golub, and Fagan studied drug users and sellers in New York City in the late 1980s and found that almost all crack users had previously been users of other illegal drugs, crack involvement was largely not related to increased nondrug criminality, and that crack use did not "appear to be associated with the initiation of violent behaviors such as assault, robbery, or rape" (1995, 280-81). Other research found that drug-related violence during the period of expanding crack markets was generally confined to inner city communities (Brownstein et al. 1992). Interestingly, Inciardi notes that even when researchers began to report that crack was a problem largely limited to inner city neighborhoods and the federal Drug Enforcement Administration announced in 1986 that crack was not a major problem in most areas of the country, the major news media continued to treat crack as a national crisis and its spread as an epidemic or even a plague (Inciardi 1992, 107).

This all suggests that the role played by policy-makers and politicians, law enforcement officials and practitioners, and the news media in the construction of the problem of crack-related violence deserves more serious attention. The crack markets were violent markets and where they were found so too was violent crime. To some extent, the rise and then fall of the official record of violent crime in the U.S. can be attributed to the invention, establishment, and evolution of crack cocaine and crack markets. However, more important to the growing measure of violence was the response to crack by those who manage public opinion and public policy.

During the 1980s, the U.S. experienced what one observer called a "justice juggernaut," a policy and program paradigm shift that moved "criminal justice ideology from the 'soft' approach of rehabilitation to the 'hard' one of deterrence, retribution, and incapacitation" (Gordon 1990, 15). Public support was needed to enact the "get tough" policies and programs that would character-ize the juggernaut. The hysteria that surrounded the alleged crack *crisis* and crack *epidemic* had what Weber would call an "elective affinity" (Gerth and Mills 1946) with the need of criminal justice and law enforcement officials to demonstrate high levels of violent crime associated with drugs in order to support the massive expansion of the criminal justice system and the loosening of restrictions on law enforcement that were central to the justice juggernaut. While the intent of officials may not have been to increase the amount of violence, it behooved them to demonstrate that there was a high level of violent crime. In that sense, the wave of violent crime defined by the UCR violent crime index was as a much a product of the efforts of these institutional claims-makers as it was the product of the youngsters who engaged in the crack market trade. The chapters that follow will examine the role of policy-makers, law enforcement officials, and the news media in contributing to the construction of the notion and reality of crack-related violence, and will consider how each used crack to support a political agenda.

4

Making Policy, Making Justice, Making Crime

Government policy-makers played an important role in the construction of the *crisis* of crack-related violence in the U.S. in the 1980s. No argument will be made that government alone can control or even influence the actual level or nature of crime. However, in its role as manufacturer and guardian of official crime statistics and maker of policy, government influences the nature and level of measured crime, as well as the public perception of crime (Brownstein 1995).

Social or cultural crises can be manufactured to generate support for other items on a political agenda. Such was the case with crack cocaine. Through a comprehensive review of the record of crack and other drug scares in the U.S., Reinarman and Levine uncovered and identified the political utility of crack cocaine. They observed that in the later years of the 1980s "the crack crisis has increased police, court, and parole system supervision of urban underclass minorities, and has made the jails and prisons bulge. All the while, unemployment, poverty, and homelessness remain untouched" (1989, 566). For the New Right, this supported a "conservative-led drive to reduce social spending" (1995, 566). For the Liberal Democrats, a crack crisis served as "a convenient scapegoat for deteriorating conditions in the inner cities—and all this at a historical moment when the liberals' traditional solutions to the problems of the poor were stigmatized by a successful Right as ineffective and costly" (1995, 566). That is, according to Reinarman and Levine, "the new chemical bogeyman afforded politicians across the ideological spectrum both an explanation for pressing public problems and an excuse for not doing much about them" (1995, 566).

Satisfying the Public Demand for Policy and Action on Crack Cocaine

With the passage of the Harrison Narcotics Act in 1914 and then the Marijuana Tax Act in 1937, drug use in the United States officially became a criminal problem (Bakalar and Grinspoon 1984; Inciardi 1992; Kaplan 1970; Musto 1973; Trebach 1982). By the later years of the twentieth century, the policy of criminalizing drug involvement was institutionalized with explicit declarations of war on drugs, first by President Richard Nixon in 1971 and then by President Ronald Reagan in 1982 (Brownstein 1992; Wisotsky 1986; Weisheit 1990). Consequently, in the middle of the 1980s, when crack was first observed on the streets of the largest U.S. cities, the foundation for a "get tough" policy in response to a new drug crisis was already in place.

George Bush was President when the federal policy toward crack cocaine evolved. Under his authority and through the newly organized Office of National Drug Control Policy (ONDCP), William Bennett directed drug policy in the United States. In the first *National Drug Control Strategy* report issued by his office, Bennett established that crack was a serious problem. He wrote, "crack use is spreading like a plague" and that "[crack] is, in fact, the most dangerous and quickly addictive drug known to man" (1989, 3). In the next report he identified what the government would do about the crack problem with the words "it is the policy of the United States to disrupt, dismantle, and ultimately destroy the illegal market for drugs" (1990, 1). The federal policy set the tone for the response in the states.

By the spring of 1986, as politicians and policy-makers in New York State and City were watching official estimates of crime and criminal violence rising, they were first made aware of crack. Other than the anecdotal accounts of street drug researchers in the city, little was known about this new drug. Nonetheless, with the support of the media, the belief that crack was somehow related to the rising level of violence took hold in the public mind. Demands for action were firm and immediate. Initially, the call was for enhanced law enforcement and more drug treatment programs. The State government responded.

In a press release dated May 5, 1986, Mario Cuomo, then Governor of New York, was quoted as saying, "Crack is an insidious new drug with all the seductive qualities of cocaine. It poses an even greater danger than traditional form of cocaine because it can create intense dependencies and psychological addition after very brief use." At that time, Cuomo, like everyone else in the nation, really knew almost nothing about crack. He was responding to public pressure and using official yet unsubstantiated statements to do so. He announced new drug law enforcement initiatives to "crack down on crack," such as enhancing the penalty for the sale of cocaine within a legislatively designated school property boundary.

In a press release dated June 17, 1986, the Governor announced that "$10 million would be devoted to new and expanded programs to prevent and treat abuse of crack and other drugs." The message to the media listed initiatives such as the distribution of pamphlets and the development of public service announcements, and concluded with the Governor saying, "I am confident these initiatives will stem the growing crack problem." Unfortunately, at that time there were no programs that were known to be successful in preventing cocaine use or in treating people who were abusing crack cocaine.

A copy of testimony delivered by Governor Cuomo to the U.S. House Select Committee on Narcotics Abuse and Control was made available to the press on July 18, 1986. In those remarks, the Governor referred to the purported epidemic proportion of what was already being called *the crack problem*. He said, "The cocaine alarm is sounding throughout the nation. There is no escape anywhere. . . . We are truly dealing with an epidemic of unprecedented proportions." In the same testimony he alluded to the addictive and crimogenic nature of crack when he referred to "dramatic increases in addiction and increases in arrest for drug-related crimes." Inadvertently, in this message the Governor suggested that the response had exceeded the knowledge about crack when he said, "Statistics for crack are new, but crack has become of such concern that the New York City Police Department has established an undercover unit of 101 officers solely to arrest dealers and break up crack houses."

Continuing to respond to public pressure for action, on August 14 the Governor reiterated the need for enhanced enforcement in crack cases in a three-page press release announcing the formation of a Statewide Drug Enforcement Task Force comprised of

"prominent officials from federal, State and local law enforcement." In addition, noting that the State was "constantly developing additional weapons against the scourge of crack and other
illegal drugs," he announced his support for legislation that would
"substantially increase the penalties for the sale of crack" and
"criminalize the monies obtained from illegal drug sales." The
Governor is quoted as saying, "We will accept nothing less than the
toughest penalties for those who would sell this addictive, destructive drug to our children." He then announced the creation of a
"new Narcotics Unit" in the State Police and "renewed his call for
additional judges."

In August, 1986, just months after the first press release on the
crack problem, on the editorial page of a publication prepared by
the New York State Governor's Office of Employee Relations,
Governor Cuomo wrote, "There is a new drug out on the streets
shattering the lives of our children and destroying the health of our
communities. That drug is called crack" (1986a, 16). The next
month in the same publication, there were two articles on crack.
One was called "Crack—The deadliest cocaine of all" (1986b).
The other had the headline, "Undercover researchers about crack
use, 'You become the living dead'" (1986b). With these reports,
the Governor was sharing the early anecdotal evidence about the
crack problem with state employees.

The government response to crack in New York was not
merely symbolic. From 1983 to 1987, felony drug arrests increased
in New York State by 118 percent, indictments by 207 percent,
convictions by 210 percent, and sentences to prison for drug
convictions by 220 percent (Ross and Cohen 1988). In 1988,
sentences to prison for drug convictions accounted for 37 percent
of all sentences to State prison (Division of Criminal Justice
Services 1988).

Research and the Internal Generation of Policy on Crack

Despite the vast number of claims about crack and the enormity of the political response, little was really known during the spring and summer of 1986. Nonetheless, the government of New York was being called upon to act forcefully. Legislators and citizen's action groups recommended legal and social policy changes favoring strict law enforcement and tougher penalties in crack-related cases.

As noted above, the story about what the government was doing in response to the crack problem as told to the public through the media was immediate and harsh. Within the government policy-making bureaucracy itself, there was some interest in information that would justify the proposals set forth to satisfy public demand. Of greater concern, however, was the government demand for information about the potential impact of these initiatives on government resources.

As public and media concern about crack cocaine continued to grow, questions continued to pour into state government research units. Responses had to come quickly. There was no time to design new studies, collect data, and then conduct analyses directed specifically at the questions being asked. Generally, researchers had to turn to existing data files, the ones routinely maintained and used to generate official crime statistics, and to personal communication with people in the field.

The first and most obvious question was: "How extensive is the crack problem?" The Street Research Unit of the New York State Division of Substance Abuse Services (DSAS), a team of ethnographers who studied the drug using and selling communities in the city, reported that the first mention they heard of crack cocaine came sometime in 1983. By June, 1986, the Narcotics Unit of the New York City Police Department (NYPD) was reporting that 53 percent of all cocaine arrests in the city involved crack, and that by July crack was involved in 74 percent of cocaine arrests and one-third of all drug arrests. The federal Drug Enforcement Administration (DEA), which made its first crack arrest in New York City in 1985, reported that during July, 1986 about one-third of DEA arrests in the city involved crack.

As staff to the Governor's Director of Criminal Justice, our office was responsible for collecting all information related to the crime and justice aspects of the crack problem. So I was asked to call the NYPD and find out how they determined whether or not a drug arrest was related to crack. I was told that from January 1 to June 19, 1986, crack arrests were counted manually. An event was counted as crack-related if it had any evidence of crack involvement. For example, an arrest was identified as crack-related if the top arrest charge or any other charge was for cocaine or crack possession or sale, if crack paraphernalia (such as the vials in which it was sold) was found at the scene, or even simply if the arresting officer indicated he or she thought crack was involved. Beginning on June 20, a special event code for crack arrests was added to the on-line booking sheet, automating the classification process but not necessarily making the definition more restrictive. From that time on, an arrest was considered crack-related only if the top charge was a cocaine drug arrest *and* the special code for crack was marked, for whatever reason.

Clearly, questions about the nature and extent of crack use and trade were not easy to answer. Nor were questions about the link between crack and crime or violence. Police departments, for example, did not routinely record information about drug involvement in individual case records. So staff of various state agencies produced numerous briefings, reports, and memoranda to try to address these questions by extrapolation from available data. For example, an observed increase in the number of officially-recorded cocaine-involved emergency room admissions was used as an indicator of the spread of crack.

There was one source of new data that directly addressed the question of how far crack had spread, though that was based on informal interviews with a nonrandom sample of known drug users. From May 7 to 28, 1986, members of the Street Research Unit of DSAS informally surveyed 241 drug users known to them from around New York City (DSAS 1986). They found that 70 percent of those sampled had used crack at one time or another. They also found that 60 percent of those who had used it paid for it with money they had acquired illegally, and that 73 percent of the crack users believed that crack had changed their lives for the worse.

Given the operational purposes of the data regularly maintained by the state, questions about the formal processing of drug users and traffickers in general were easier to address. By August, 1986, DCJS had produced a formal report called *Criminal Sale of Controlled Substances: Analysis of Criminal Justice Processing* (Albert and Harig 1986). By September of that year a companion report on the processing of *Criminal Possession* was released (Albert 1986). These reports showed, for example, that the number of arrests for the sale and possession of a controlled substance rose by 121 percent from 1981 to 1985. However alarming they might have been, these statistics said more about the system response to drugs than about the problem of drugs itself, and they really said nothing at all about crack cocaine.

Policy-Making and the Definition of the Crack Problem

In his annual address to the New York State Legislature in January, 1987, just after his election to a second term of office, Governor Cuomo defined the crack problem for the State. He told state legislators:

> This year, we must intensify our efforts as never before in the
> face of the emergence of crack—the extraordinarily potent,
> highly addictive and relatively inexpensive cocaine
> derivative. The lightning speed with which this lethal drug
> has spread through society is evident in substantial increases
> in drug-related deaths and demands for treatment by drug
> users. Crack has also been accompanied by rising incidents
> of violent crime, including robberies and murders. We must
> attack this new menace by enacting stiffer penalties for its
> sale and possession. (1987, 39)

This statement effectively became the official government definition of the crack problem in New York. The problem had been constructed on the basis of a particular set of assumptions that could not be verified by research or experience, though they all had been objectified in the public imagination by earlier government announcements and media reports. These included the belief that crack was particularly lethal and addictive, that crack use had reached epidemic proportion, that crack was largely responsible for the increasing level of violent crime, and that the appropriate policy response to crack was enhanced enforcement of drug laws (Brownstein 1991a).

By January, 1989, public fear and concern about crack was still high, but it was old news in New York. The Governor announced a "Campaign Against Drug Abuse." In his annual message to the State Legislature that year he opened his remarks by telling those present that the three most serious problems facing New Yorkers were "drugs, drugs and drugs" (Cuomo 1989). Note that he did not say, "crack, crack and crack." He then used the same forum to announce the formation of a Statewide Anti-Drug Abuse Council (ADAC), to be headed by the Lieutenant Governor, Stan Lundine. The mission of this Council was to develop a statewide strategy to deal with the drug problem in general; crack would be a prominent theme, though not the only one. In its first annual report published at the end of 1989, there was a listing of 110 recommendations. Of these, 41 were oriented to law enforcement, 38 to prevention, and 31 to treatment (ADAC 1989).

A year later, at the end of 1990, the second annual ADAC strategy report included the following statement: "A significant body of evidence exists [official crime statistics were presented as the evidence in the report pages that followed] telling us that while substantial gains have been made in addressing New York's drug and alcohol abuse problem, the problems persist at an unacceptable level" (1990, 3). Notably, as the Governor did in his 1989 address to the State Legislature, this report had shifted the focus from crack alone to drugs and alcohol in general.

Policy-Making and the Construction of the Crisis of Crack and Violence

In essence, policy-making is a process of prioritization and resource allocation (Brownstein 1991b). The makers of policy make decisions and take actions that identify and define the problems of their jurisdiction and determine the type and level of resources that will be devoted to the solution of those problems. As politicians, it is to their advantage to select problems they have the ability and will to solve, or at least those on which they may be perceived by the public as having a positive impact. As claims-makers competing in what Best called the "social problems marketplace" (1990, 15), it is also to their advantage to use their position as political insiders to divert attention and resources to those problems over which they have ownership and control and therefore have a greater ability to manage (Brownstein 1995).

In the later years of the 1980s, crack-related violence was a good problem for U.S. policy-makers. The difficult and intractable problems of the economy and the social structure—problems like unemployment and poverty, social welfare and homelessness, education and illiteracy, inequality and injustice—could be set aside while policy-makers devoted their attention to crack cocaine and the violence that appeared to be its companion.

Crack-related violence was well-suited to this purpose. Drug scares have a long history in the U.S. of diverting public attention from other more difficult and more durable problems (Bakalar and Grinspoon 1984; Duster 1970; Inciardi 1992; Musto 1973; Reinarman and Levine 1989). Traditionally, these periods of panic or hysteria about one or another drug have served to draw attention to individuals, usually victims, as the source of social problems. As Reinarman and Levine wrote about the crack scare in particular and drug scares in general, they are "the product of the association of 'dangerous drugs' with a 'dangerous class'" (1989, 555). Once individuals have been determined to be the problem, policies and programs can be developed that separate those individuals from the rest of society, something relatively easy to do when compared to changing economic or social structural conditions.

Crack thus served policy-makers as a device for shifting the blame for the social problems of the time from the decisions and actions of government and the conditions of social and economic institutions to the deviance of individuals, specifically those individuals who used and trafficked in crack cocaine. In their analysis of the context of the crack crisis, Reinarman and Levine observed that given the ideological agenda of the Republican New Right, the fit was perfect. Crack was used "as an ideological fig leaf to place over the unsightly urban ills that had increased markedly under [President Ronald] Reagan administration social and fiscal policies" (1989, 561-2). Specifically, "Unemployment, poverty, urban decay, school crises, crime, and all their attendant forms of human troubles were spoken of and acted upon as if they were the result of *individual* deviance, immorality, or weakness" (Reinarman and Levine 1989, 561).

In terms of criminal justice policy, the 1980s in the U.S. was a period of enormous system expansion accompanied by a philosophical shift from rehabilitation to enforcement (Gordon 1990). Without crack, this probably would not have been possible. Even with incorrect or at best insufficient information about the drug and its impact (Brownstein 1991a; Johnson, Golub, and Fagan 1995; Klein and Maxson 1994), criminal justice policy-makers in the U.S. in the 1980s were able to generate public fear about the dangers of crack and crack-related violence that permitted the creation and mobilization of what Gordon called "the justice juggernaut" (1990). By supporting the notion that crack was driving the level of criminal violence to new heights, policy-makers were able to enact a political agenda that diverted resources from social welfare programs to criminal enforcement programs, and to define the social problems of the times in terms that made them appear to be more manageable by government. Put simply, in the United States in the 1980s, policy-makers were well-served by high rates of violent crime.

5

Law Enforcement and Crime Construction

In a sense, William Bratton was correct when he spoke to the criminologists in attendance at the Boston meeting in 1995. Law enforcement programs and practices did contribute to the decline in the UCR-measured violent crime rate in New York City that began in 1990. But certainly not only and perhaps not even necessarily for the reasons he suggested. The relationship between law enforcement and the level of crime in a community is complex. The impact of law enforcement on crime is likely to be both direct and indirect, intended and unintended. Law enforcement programs and practices most likely *are* related to the nature and level of crime (President's Commission 1968). Concurrently, however, law enforcement policies and procedures contribute to the official measure of crime, which after all is a social construction of police knowledge and action in response to specified behaviors.

This chapter focuses on the policies, programs, and practices of law enforcement agencies designed to deal with violent crime when it first began to rise in the early 1980s and when it began to fall after 1990. Special attention is given to the programs that were initiated in response to the violence associated with crack cocaine, including both the street enforcement programs that were introduced when crack-related violence appeared to be increasing and the community-oriented policing programs that emerged with the apparent decline in that violence. Both the intended and unintended consequences of these programs will be considered in the context of the vested interest of law enforcement agencies in the level of violent crime.

Police Policies and Practices in Response to Crack-Related Violence

The government of the U.S. responded to the violence associated with crack cocaine by increasing funding and support for law enforcement. With the emphasis of the Office of National Drug Control Policy under William Bennett on the disruption and destruction of illegal drug markets (ONDCP 1990, 1), federal support for law enforcement programs that addressed drug-related crime and violence expanded. By the end of the 1980s, approximately 70 percent of all federal dollars allocated to drug-related problems were designated for law enforcement or interdiction programs (Office of National Drug Control Policy 1989, 1990; Senate Judiciary Committee 1990).

Street-Level Enforcement. During the 1970s, the favored strategy of drug law enforcement agencies was to build cases against middle level or upper level drug dealers (Moore 1977). By the early 1980s, interest shifted to the arrest of lower level dealers and users through programs that consolidated tactics such as buy and bust operations, undercover surveillance, and stakeouts (Chaiken 1988; Hayeslip 1989; Moore and Kleiman 1989; Sherman 1990).

Just prior to the introduction of crack cocaine to drug users in the U.S., a street-level law enforcement strategy was developed to disrupt the heroin trade in urban communities (Kleiman 1986, 1988; Zimmer 1987). This strategy was based on a saturation model of policing in which large numbers of police officers would be assigned to a specific area for a specific period of time to interdict the movement of drugs into the area, disrupt street sales, and to arrest drug users and traffickers.

Early evaluations of the saturation programs suggested a potential for success. In his evaluation of a program in Lynn, Massachusetts, Kleiman concluded that "increased enforcement pressure tended to decrease heroin use" and that there was a significant decline in the level of street crime in the area both during and following the saturation period (1988, 6). Kleiman did acknowledge an obvious limitation of his finding, noting that Lynn, Massachusetts represents "one extreme among drug markets—small, concentrated, isolated" (1988, 15). The other extreme, "big, cosmopolitan, and in a city with thriving drug markets in several other neighborhoods" (Kleiman 1988, 15), was represented by the Lower East Side of New York City. Operation Pressure Point, a pilot program begun in New York in 1984 to deal with the thriving heroin trade, was found to have resulted in a reduction of heroin dealing and violent crime in the area (Kleiman 1988; Zimmer 1987).

Other evaluations of saturation programs from the early 1980s reported lesser success and even failure of the model to reduce heroin trade or heroin-related crime. In Lawrence, Massachusetts, heroin sales did decline, but apparently because users found an alternative supply across the county line in Lowell (Kleiman 1988, 17). In addition, the Lawrence program failed to produce a reduction in the level of property crime in the area. "Operation Cold Turkey" in Philadelphia was closed by public protest and legal action after only four days of operation (Kleiman 1988, 18).

Nonetheless, interest in the saturation model grew and eventually became irresistible when the public demand to do something about crack and crack-related violence reached its height in the middle of the 1980s (Smith et al. 1992). Following the killing of a police officer by a drug dealer in New York City, the New York City Police Department (NYPD) responded in 1988 with its Tactical Narcotics Team (TNT) program. TNT was "[d]esigned to provide a short-term 'concentrated overlay' of street level drug enforcement in a narrowly defined target area [by supplementing] existing narcotics operations with intensive 'buy and bust' activity, focusing primarily on crack sales, but also addressing powdered cocaine and heroin trafficking" (Hillsman et al. 1989).

Violence as an Unintended Consequence. Early critics of street enforcement efforts expressed a number of concerns about the ability of the saturation programs to accomplish their goals. A major concern involved the notion of "displacement," which suggests that "crimes might diminish in a community after a crackdown not because they have been averted, but because they have been shifted elsewhere" (Barnett 1988, 40). Similarly, concern was expressed about the quality of arrests under such programs. Bouza suggested that "[while] street enforcement results in more arrests, fewer prosecutions are successful" (1988, 45).

In a more recent study of targeted police raids of crack houses as "hot spots" of criminal activity, Sherman and Rogan and their associates validated at least one of these concerns (1995). They found a modest deterrent effect "of block-level crime and disorder," but concluded that this effect would "decay" and then "disappear" quickly and, in any case, "may be mitigated by displacement" (Sherman, Rogan, and others 1995, 776).

An evaluation of TNT by the Vera Institute using both statistical and ethnographic research methods did not necessarily justify the early concerns, but it did demonstrate that people who participated in the crack markets located in target areas "adapted to the intensive enforcement activity in a variety of ways" (Smith et al. 1992, 141). The dealers adapted "by moving selling locations indoors, by shifting selling hours to times when it was believed that TNT might not be operating, by devising schemes to reduce hand-to-hand exchanges, by moving out of the selling location after a sale, by using 'observers' adept at spotting TNT vehicles, and by reducing the volume of outdoor sales for the duration of the intervention" (Smith et al. 1992, 141). In addition, the evaluation found no evidence of reduced criminal activity in the targeted area.

In terms of the potential impact of law enforcement programs on the violence associated with the crack trade, perhaps the most important finding of the Vera Institute evaluation of TNT was that "many [curbside crack sellers who were arrested under the TNT program] were quickly replaced by other user-dealers" (Smith et al. 1992, 141). In an earlier chapter of this book it was demonstrated that much of the crack-related violence was the product of the instability of the early crack markets, with young and inexperienced independent drug dealers confronting one another in disputes over territorial and financial claims. The violence declined as these markets became more stable. When a law enforcement program such as TNT arrests the low level crack dealer selling from a particular sales spot, the program effectively disrupts whatever order has been established at that spot (compare, Reuter 1991, 147). The arrested dealer must abandon the spot where he or she had established control, and any number of other young entrepreneurs are then free to compete for the spot. Given the crowded condition of the courts and jails, before long the original dealer is likely to be back on the street, ready to do battle for the rights to his or her old territory. That is, saturation programs themselves were a potential source of increased rather than decreased crack-related violence.

Police Policies and Practices as Violent Crime Declined

One of the more interesting though collateral findings of the Vera Institute's evaluation of TNT was that "both community leaders and street-level respondents expressed a preference for a more community-oriented style of policing, in contrast to the enforcement-heavy TNT approach" (Sviridoff and Hillsman 1994, 125). Police officers may not necessarily have shared the enthusiasm of the people living in the communities where crack markets flourished, but the time for community-based policing had arrived.

The Focus on Community. While the role of the police in a democratic society is complex and multifaceted, the defining responsibility of police authority has always been the maintenance of social order (Goldstein 1993; Skolnick 1966; Task Force on the Police 1967; Wilson 1971). In the middle of the 1960s, a period of urban unrest in the United States, the federal government formally concluded through its Task Force on the Police that any community's "ability to maintain stability and to solve its problems" was dependent on the establishment of working relationships between the police and the residents of that community (1967, 144). Thus were planted the roots for the contemporary incarnation of community-based policing as a strategy for dealing with problems of law and order.

Community Policing. Community policing is easy to conceptualize. According to Skolnick and Bayley, "The central premise of community policing is that the public should play a more active and coordinated role in enhancing safety. The police cannot bear the responsibility alone, nor can the criminal justice system" (1988, 3; see also Kratcoski and Dukes 1995; Trojanowicz and Bucqueroux 1990). However, as simple as it is to conceptualize, it is difficult to define community policing in practical terms for purposes of implementation.

Trojanowicz and Bucqueroux defined community policing as "a new philosophy of policing, based on the concept that police officers and private citizens working together in creative ways can help to solve contemporary community problems related to crime, fear of crime, social and physical disorder, and neighborhood decay" (1990, 5). Beyond its emphasis on cooperation and order, how does this philosophy translate into practice? Mastrofski, Worden, and Snipes suggest that there are at least three distinct models of community policing (1995).

Problem-oriented policing "asks line officers to use their heads, to look for the underlying dynamics behind a series of incidents, rather than to focus on the individual occurrences as isolated events" (Trojanowicz and Bucqueroux 1990, 8). For example, after a visit by the Secretary of Housing and Urban Development in 1989 to number of public housing developments, the conclusion was reached that "crime and vandalism, long endemic in public housing, have been significantly exacerbated by drug abuse, and particularly by the crack epidemic that swelled in mid-1980's" (Dunworth and Saiger 1994, iii). Consequently, drugs having been defined as the underlying dynamic, federal funds were made available for drug control programs in selected public housing projects as a way to address the problem of crime and violence generally.

The second approach identified by Mastrofski and his associates is "community building," which they suggest places the emphasis of the police on "crime prevention [and] victim assistance" to build positive relationships and rapport between the police and residents of the community (1995, 540). For example, to drive drug dealers from the Fairlawn area of Washington, D.C. in the late 1980s, police and citizens walked together at night as a deterrence to drug traffickers (Weingart, Hartmann, and Osborne 1994, 3-4).

The third model, "broken windows," is the approach to community policing that William Bratton and others have suggested worked in New York City to reduce the rising level of violent crime in the city at the end of the era of expanding crack cocaine markets.

Broken Windows. When Rudolph Giuliani became Mayor of New York City, he selected William Bratton to head the City's police department because the two shared a common belief that clearing the city of minor offense violators would result in a reduced level of major offenses. As Giuliani told one news reporter, "'I chose Bill Bratton,' says Giuliani, 'because he agreed with the Broken Windows theory'" (Pooley 1996, 56).

In 1982, before the introduction of crack cocaine but after a number of urban communities in the U.S. had re-assigned police officers to foot patrol to improve the quality of life in those areas, Wilson and Kelling introduced the notion of "broken windows" to law enforcement. They argued:

> . . . vandalism can occur anywhere once communal barriers—
> the sense of mutual regard and the obligations of civility—
> are lowered by actions that seem to signal that 'no one
> cares.' . . . We suggest that 'untended' behavior also leads to
> the breakdown of community controls. A stable
> neighborhood of families who care for their homes, mind
> each other's children, and confidently frown on unwanted
> intruders can change, in a few years or even a few months, to
> an inhospitable and frightening jungle. . . . At this time it is
> not inevitable that serious crime will flourish or violent
> attacks on strangers will occur. But many residents will think
> that crime, especially violent crime, is on the rise, and they
> will modify their behavior accordingly. (1982, 31-32)

This explanation suggests two important points about the

broken windows approach. First, the residents of a community that sets standards for itself and adheres to those standards will enjoy an acceptable level of public order. Second, the perception of crime is at least as important to people as is the actual level of crime, and restoring the quality of life to a community makes the people in that community believe that they are safer and more secure, whether or not they really are.

In New York City in July 1984, the New York City Police Department implemented a "community-oriented, problem-solving policing program" called the Community Patrol Officer Program or CPOP (McElroy, Cosgrove, and Sadd 1993, 6). The purpose of New York's version of community policing was "to enhance the quality of life in the many neighborhoods that make up the City of New York" (McElroy, Cosgrove, and Sadd 1993, 196).

CPOP was started by Police Commissioner Lee Brown under Mayor Ed Koch, and was grounded in the broken windows approach, based on concerns for quality of life and order maintenance. Next, the additional police officers to support the program were hired by Commissioner Raymond Kelly under Mayor David Dinkins. But it was Bratton under Giuliani who truly operationalized the broken windows model. According to one account, "Giuliani instructed Bratton to do something Dinkins would never have allowed: use those [additional] cops to crack down on minor offenders, public drunks, potheads, those who urinate on the street, aggressive panhandlers, graffiti scribblers and 'squeegee pests,' who converged on cars at stoplights to clean windshields for spare change" (Poole 1996, 56). As official crime rates declined, Giuliani and Bratton took credit, despite the fact that the decline actually began in the last year of Dinkins' term as Mayor.

Since taking office as Police Commissioner of New York City in January 1994, William Bratton watched his reputation grow in the face of continuously declining official levels of crime. Of course crime was declining in most large cities in the nation, but

New York has always been the national symbol of crime, so the trend there was that much more noticeable. Maybe too noticeable. In April 1996, Giuliani had Bratton removed from office (Beals and Thomas 1996, 42) and the Mayor declared his new plan to crush "drug trafficking and the drug business" (Krauss 1996, B1).

The Utility of Community Policing for Managing Drug-Related Violent Crime. A variety of questions have been asked about community policing. Typically they are questions of implementation. Is it better to have "no community policing at all than the limp, watered down versions that serve up only thin gruel of citizen participation" (Mastrofski and Greene 1993)? Is community policing merely an exercise in "public relations" (Ross 1995)? Does community policing impact on the arrest patterns of police officers (Mastrofski, Worden, and Snipes 1995)?

The broken windows approach to community policing raises another question for crime prevention and control, one that asks about impact. If the broken windows in a community are repaired, will crime in the community decline? That is a central assumption of the model (Wilson and Kelling 1982). In New York City, the official level of crime did decline when the police began working with communities to restore order. But others things happened as well, such as the evolution of the crack cocaine markets, and it is not possible to say with certainty that violent crime came down simply or even primarily because the police repaired the broken windows.

Police Commissioner Bratton did succeed in making people believe that crime was declining and that they were safer. However, for two reasons his success may not have been as substantial as it appeared on the surface to be. First, even Wilson and Kelling acknowledged that fixing broken windows is better at making people feel that they are safer than it is at actually reducing levels of crime (1982, 31). Second, it was to the Commissioner's advantage as a police official to demonstrate that crime was declining under his watch. That is, he had a program that was known to create in citizens a sense that their communities were safer, and he had a vested interest in demonstrating that the level of crime had been reduced.

The Police and the Construction of Violent Crime

In the marketplace of social problems (Best 1990), political insiders are in a position to use official statistics to make claims that support or even shift resources to their favored social policies and programs (Brownstein 1995). When they participate in the social construction of those statistics, their ability to make such claims is enhanced, as in the case of local police agencies and the official crime statistics, the Uniform Crime Reports. This is not to say that police agencies intentionally tamper with the levels of crime to support claims about the efficacy of particular programs or policies, either programmatically or by statistical manipulation. But it does remind us that for a variety of reasons, sometimes unclear even to the officials involved, crime statistics vary independent of the actual level of crime. Notably, internal interpretations, decisions, and actions have significant impacts on what is reported as crime and how much of it is reported.

The impact on the level of crime that is related to law enforcement programs and practices is obvious. Theoretically, police programs and practices should not be designed or implemented to increase the level of crime in a community. There is no evidence that police departments would strive for that end, even if it were in their own interest. Nonetheless, there are law enforcement programs and policies that have the unintended consequence of increasing the level of crime. One example is the street-enforcement approach that was used to destroy crack cocaine markets in the late 1980s. As indicated earlier, there is evidence that those programs actually drove the drug dealing indoors, where sellers and buyers did not have even the minimal protection of public view, and inadvertently and repeatedly disrupted volatile drug markets that were otherwise stabilizing as a result of normal market forces.

Less obvious is the impact on the publicly accepted level of crime as defined by official crime statistics. Through its role in the manufacture of those statistics, law enforcement has an obvious impact on the level and nature of violent crime. UCR statistics are the product of the observations and recordings of local police agencies. What is observed, what is defined as crime, and what is officially recorded as crime are subject to policy and program interpretations and decisions by police officials, and to the discretion and practice of police officers. In a recent comparison of UCR violent crime statistics and National Crime Victimization Survey statistics for the years 1973 to 1992, years surrounding the rise and fall of the official record of violent crime around the introduction and evolution of crack markets, O'Brien found evidence for the "hypothesis that police productivity explains the sharp rise in UCR violent crime rates over this period" (1996, 204). He concludes, "If I am correct, the 20-year period from 1973 to 1992 was not a period of ever-increasing rates of violent crime. Instead it was a period of ever-increasing police productivity in terms of the recording of crimes that occurred" (O'Brien 1996, 204).

When crack cocaine markets were expanding and violent crime could be associated with that expansion, federal and state agencies were shifting resources to programs directed at reducing drug-related violence. It was therefore advantageous for local police agencies to demonstrate high levels of drug-related violent crime in their jurisdictions to improve their chances of getting the state and federal dollars. When the governments providing the increased funding raised the question of what was working, it was to the advantage of local police agencies to demonstrate that their programs were working, so that support would continue. As the interest in the issue of drugs and violence waned, then the value of high violent crime rates for local police agencies diminished. While crime rates may rise and fall for a number of reasons, the interests of the agencies that participate in the construction of those statistics cannot be ignored.

Epilogue

In November of 1992, when the level of violent crime was already dropping in New York City, the New York State Police released a study that found, according to area news reports, "Menacing drug gangs from New York City are responsible for increasing violence in inner-city neighborhoods in Albany and other upstate urban communities" (Mahoney 1992, A1). The report itself blamed the problem on TNT, arguing, "As pressure was exerted on street dealers in New York City by Tactical Narcotics Teams, narcotics traffickers moved to more lucrative upstate markets, bringing increasing levels of violent crime with them" (Constantine 1992, 1).

Schenectady, New York is a city of about 65,000 people just west of Albany, the state capital. The people of Schenectady, especially those living in the inner city neighborhood of Hamilton Hill, heard the alarming news, observed the drugs and crime in their neighborhood, and, according to the State Police, asked for help. Six o'clock one Wednesday morning in the middle of November, a year after the State Police report was released, Operation Crackdown came to their rescue. Under the direction of the State Police and the lights of a helicopter flying overhead, "black trucks" unloaded 540 "heavily armed" police officers from the city and surrounding region who "stormed the city in teams of four to 12 with a force never before seen in this region" (McGlone 1993, A1). By 9 o'clock that evening, 85 people had been arrested and jailed and the force had "confiscated two loaded shotguns, a loaded revolver, about four ounces of cocaine, about $1,200 in cash and some drug paraphernalia" (McGlone 1993, A4). According to news accounts, "residents cheered" the army of policemen "[c]lad in black and wearing black military-style helmets and carrying large black shields" (Mahoney 1993, A1).

The police had saved the day and the media were there to tell the story. By 1993, the media had gotten quite good at telling the story of crack and violence.

6

Telling and Selling the Story of Crack, Crime, and Violence

The primary social function of the news media as a social institution is and always has been public information (Lee 1973). However, news reporting today is also an industry, the primary function of which is economic—to earn a profit (Koch 1990; Lee 1973; Mayer 1987). Consequently, news today is constructed in a political economic context and "news reporting is as likely to sensationalize events as it is to report them, as likely to serve as an instrument of propaganda as it is to be a source of information, and as iikely to be a creator of myth as it is to be a purveyor of truth"

(Brownstein 1991a, 86; also, compare Barak 1988; Koch 1990; Lee 1978; Lee and Lee 1939; McCarthy, McPhail, and Smith 1996).

The news media in the United States in the late 1980s could not ignore the story of the dramatic rise in the official record of violent crime. Nor could the media industry ignore the captivating story of crack cocaine, the expansion of crack markets, and especially the apparent spread of crack-related violence. These were stories that were in the interest of the media as an industry and of newsmakers as reporters to tell. First, they were the kind of stories that attract public attention and therefore sell news and, perhaps more important to the newsmaking industry, advertising. Further, they were stories being promoted by government policy-makers and law enforcement officials, people on whom the news media depend for the information needed to write stories. So it behooved media officials and news reporters to tell these stories about crack and violent crime.

This chapter is about the way the story of violent crime and its relationship to the evolution of crack cocaine markets was told by the news media in the U.S. during the waning decades of the twentieth century. Specifically, attention will be given to the way in which the media as an industry constructed the story in the context of its own interests, and in support of the interests of the government policy-makers and law enforcement officials who serve as the gate keepers to much of the information that reporters need to write their stories.

Reporting Crime Statistics To and Through the Media

When I was responsible for the Uniform Crime Reports program in New York State, I was always struck by the extent to which we, like the FBI on the federal level and the New York City

Police Department on the local level, orchestrated the release of crime statistics in relation to the rhythms of the news industry. For example, the order of release among the various agencies, the news worthiness of the day of the week and the time of the day, and the other crime stories making news at the same time were all taken into consideration before the decision to release the statistics was made. Naturally, we were dependent on when the numbers were available for calculation and hence reporting, but nothing was ever released without the processing and approval of the agency press office.

When statistical tables were prepared for release, we would give them to the agency Public Information Officer (PIO) along with our explanation for them. Sometimes this was done in the form of a draft press release. Then the PIO would prepare his or her own draft release that put the numbers in the context of agency and government policy. We were asked to review that draft, but only for accuracy of the numbers reported. The PIO and the Commissioner would determine the meaning that they wanted to be attached to the statistics, the PIO would revise the release so that reporters would most likely read the story the way they wanted it to be read, and the Commissioner would then authorize release. My staff and I, along with all other researchers, statisticians, and policy analysts at the agency, were explicitly prohibited from speaking directly to the press.

The idea of involving the press office was to maximize the likelihood that the public would be told the story in a way that was most favorable to the agency and the government. If crime was up, it had to be clear that it was going up in spite of the best efforts of government. Better still, if not for the efforts of government, crime would have gone even higher. (That was one of my favorites.) If crime was down, of course it was the result of government policies and programs. (That was a favorite of the policy-makers, who always needed to be cautioned to avoid taking credit for the ebb and flow of crime; if you take responsibility for decreases, later you are likely to be held accountable for the inevitable increases.)

Working around the cycle of the FBI reporting program, preliminary national crime statistics for the previous year are typically released in the springtime, and final statistics are released in the fall. State agencies usually release their statistics as soon as possible after the federal statistics are released. However, local agencies invariably have something tentative to offer at the very end or beginning of each year. The numbers are theirs and it is their prerogative to do so.

The news media have always found the progression to a new calendar year to be reason to recount events and to give meaning to whatever transpired over the previous twelve months. Consequently, they welcome the tentative reports of local police agencies as reason to interpret the significance of crime statistics for the previous and coming year. To learn what meanings were given by the media to the years of rising crime rates during the later 1980s and to the subsequent years of declining crime rates through the 1990s, my Graduate Assistant, George Payer, and I searched the Lexis-Nexis database for news accounts about crime in *The New York Times* and *The Washington Post* for the period December 14 to January 15 for the years 1985 to 1996. In addition, I reviewed news accounts I had collected for other purposes from those and other sources for the years 1986 to 1996.

It should be kept in mind that the people who report the news only know what they learn from the information that is available to them, particularly from the people who provide them with information. In the case of crime statistics, those providers are necessarily government (federal, state, and local) policy-makers and law enforcement officials. Consequently, the media reports of crime and violence are interpretations of interpretations, and are limited by what they are told. Naturally, there is a certain advantage to both the providers of the information and the reporters of the stories to work cooperatively to tell each story in a way that is supportive of their own or mutual interests.

Highlighting the Rising Violence

The story of rising violent crime might be easy to sell, but it is not so easy to tell. Nationally, the official violent crime rate began to rise sharply in 1985. The rise was not consistent, however, for all jurisdictions nor for all types of violent crime. Further, it was not supported by a comparable rise in the officially recorded level of violent victimization. So the news media was in a position of having to tell a highly marketable story with caution, using a variety of footnotes and caveats.

The simple part was to point to the increase in violent crime statistics. At first, however, there was not much to say. Violent crime had been going down in the early 1980s, so a modest increase for one or two years was nothing to get excited about. The earliest stories, especially those told before crack cocaine became even a subplot, tended to say little and to explain away the increase as nothing to worry about.

On January 15, 1986, for example, *The Washington Post* ran a story on page C2 of its Metro section called, "Arlington Crime Rose 2.4% in 1985." The story was told in a dispassionate tone.

> The number of serious crimes reported in Arlington County rose 2.4 percent from 1984 to 1985, reversing a trend of declining crime rates in recent years, according to statistics released yesterday by police. Police said the increase in serious crimes—murder, robbery, aggravated assault, burglary, larceny and vehicle theft—from 7,599 to 7,781 in part may be a result of growth in the county and reflects regular cycles in the crime rate.

The account was local, violence was not highlighted, and the increase was explained as routine. The story was buried deep inside the newspaper.

Once crack became part of the story, the coverage shifted to violent crime, especially homicide, the focus was on the national problem, and the reports moved closer to the lead. On January 15, 1987, *The New York Times* ran a story through its National Desk on page 14 of Section A. The reporter wrote:

> Homicides in some of the nation's largest cities rose sharply last year as officials grappled with an increase in shootings among teen-agers and the seemingly intractable spread of cocaine and its derivative, crack. The crime rates are the highest they have been since the mid-1970's, when some cities recorded their highest rates ever.

In this account, the story of rising violent crime had been made more important, and crack had become a part of the narrative.

By the end of the decade, when the official violent crime rate reached as high as it would go in New York City and was near its apex in the nation as well, the story of rising violent crime had reached the headlines. *New York Magazine*, for example, had a Special Report in its September 3, 1990 edition called "All About Crime" (Greenberg 1990). The author wrote, "A new tidal wave of crime has swept over New York, adding terrifying numbers and stories to a city already plagued by violence" (Greenberg 1990, 20). Similarly, on September 17, 1989, *Time* magazine gave its cover to the words, "The Rotting of the Big Apple." Inside, an article called "The Decline of New York" had the subheading "A surge of brutal killings has shaken the Big Apple to its core" (Attinger 1989, 36). Thus was constructed the social and historical significance of the problem of rising violence.

The Story of Declining Violence

In 1991, Christopher Jencks wrote an article for *The American Prospect* called, "Behind the Numbers—Is Violent Crime Increas-

ing?" At that time not even New York City had begun to experience
a persistent and impressive decline in its violent crime rate. So
Jencks wrote:

> The mass media also have a very selective approach to crime
> statistics. When crime declines, as it did in the early 1980s,
> editors assume the decline is only temporary and give it very
> little air time. When crime increases, as it did in the late
> 1980s, both journalists and editors see the increase as a
> portent of things to come and give it a lot of play. (1991, 99)

Jencks could not have known. Even the media experts were
not prepared for the story about crime statistics that was just about
to unfold.

By the early 1990s, the decline in crime and violence was
becoming a story that the media was interested in telling, especially in big cities like New York. Official crime statistics do not
follow the same pattern in all communities, so the earliest accounts
naturally had a local orientation. For example, On December 20,
1993, on the first page of Section B of *The New York Times* was a
101-word article called "Suburban Crime." Simply, it said, "The
crime rate in four suburban counties—Hudson, N.J., Westchester,
N.Y., Nassau, L.I. and Fairfield, Conn.—in the New York region
a year ago dropped to its lowest level in four years, according to the
F.B.I.'s index crime statistics. . . . The suburban figures show a
pattern similar to New York City's: Reported crimes moved to
record heights in 1989 or 1990, then fell off slightly in the last two
years." Whatever the specific content of these accounts, they were
merely reporting statistics.

By the middle of the 1990s, when crime statistics had been
declining steadily and strikingly in cities like New York, the story
that Christopher Jencks said would not be told was being told all
over. On November 19, 1995 on page 12 of *The Boston Sunday
Globe*, the headline read, "Major crimes show 3-year decline—
Juvenile arrests climb 7% in US as violence drops in big cities, FBI

says." On December 31, 1995 on page A8 of the Sunday edition of *The Washington Post*, the headline read, "In a Reversal, U.S. Homicide Numbers Fall." That same day *The New York Times* had a front page story that ran 1,427 words under the headline, "New York Sees Steepest Decline in Violent Crime Rate Since '72." No longer were the reports simply accounts of statistics. Now they were truly stories, with full details and elaborate explanations. The stories referred to things like demographics, drug markets, and police strategies and tried to relate these things to the crime statistics.

On the editorial page of *The Washington Post* on January 20, 1996, the editors explained a drop in the homicide rate in the District as follows: "The downturn in murders can be chalked up to better training and deployment of homicide detectives, increased federal law enforcement help, tougher gun laws and more community support." On May 6, 1996, *The Washington Post* tried to explain the national as well as the local statistics in an article on page A9 called "Reported Serious Crime Drops for the 4th Straight Year." Under an Associated Press byline, that article said, "In addition to citing the aging of baby boomers, experts and officials attributed the four-year crime decline to closer police work with citizens, longer prison sentences for violent criminals, crackdowns on illegal guns, declining unemployment and rising public intolerance for crime." The *New York Post* on May 14, 1996 on page 46 asked the question of why, when other crimes of violence were declining in number, were there more rapes than the year before in New York City. An editorial on January 15, 1996 in *The Sun* of Baltimore posed the question: "Down goes the crime rate— Why?" The question in Baltimore is almost ironic, since, as the headline on the first page of the December 30, 1995 edition of *The Sun* reads, "Violent crime in Md. Rising—New state statistics defy national trend of less lawbreaking."

Five years after Jencks said the story of the decline of

crime would not be told, on the evening of June 7, 1996, the television news program "Dateline NBC" had as its major story the decline of crime in New York City. The reporter, Lisa Rudolph, identified the story as remarkable: New York City, "crime capital of the U.S.," had experienced a steady and dramatic decline in crime. The city was no longer the poster child for violent crime. She spoke to the Mayor and the outgoing Police Commissioner and they both smiled and told her that the city is safer now than it has been since 1970. They both pointed to their approach of starting with "quality of life crimes," what has been called elsewhere "fixing broken windows." The Police Commissioner mocked the crime experts who said it could not be done, comparing them to the people who laughed at Christopher Columbus when he said the world was round. One of those experts, Jeff Fagan of Columbia University, was interviewed. He pointed out that the decline actually began before either Mayor Giuliani or Police Commissioner Bratton had taken office, saying "They took a ball that was rolling down hill and gave it a good push." Nonetheless, for the media the story of declining crime and violence had become a good one to tell, and an easy one to sell. Also, they could tell it in a way that was supportive of the interests of the people who gave them the information about crime statistics, government policy-makers and law enforcement officials.

Selling the Story of Crack and Violence

In the late 1980s, the news media in the U.S., provided support for the notion that crime and violence were associated with crack cocaine use and trade. They effectively argued that increased crime and violence was caused by crack involvement, and that crack along with its related violence was spreading from inner city neighborhoods and minority populations to the outer city and suburbs and was increasingly a threat to all people (Brownstein

1991a). These notions were not supported by empirical evidence, but by proclaiming them to be true, the media did manage to frighten the public and thereby support the efforts of government policy-makers and law enforcement officials to get tough with crack-related crime and violence.

On August 1, 1986, *The New York Times* reported, in an article called "Rise in Major Crimes in City Continues, Police Report," that crime was up in the city and that "police officials yesterday attributed many of the increases in reported murders, robberies, and other crimes to drugs, particularly the rapid proliferation over the past several months of crack, a potent cocaine derivative." Thus the media had concluded that there was a link between violent crime and crack and, initially at least, had attributed their conclusion to "police officials." By the time the rate of violent crime reached its peak, however, the media began to report the linkage as if it were a proven fact. On December 30, 1988, for example, the New York *Daily News* in its year-end crime summary linked crack to the record number of homicides in the city that year in an article called, "Crack Whips Killing Toll." A January 16, 1989 *Newsweek* article called "A Tide of Drug Killing" stated that crack was "uniquely evil."

Once the link between crack and violent crime was firmly established as given, the media developed its own theme, one that would both draw the attention of readers and advertisers and also support the argument of government policy-makers and law enforcement officials that the solution to the problem of growing violence was to do battle with crack cocaine. Specifically, the media constructed the notion that crack-related violence was random in the sense that all people were equally at risk of victimization (Brownstein 1991a). In an article on page B1 in *The New York Times* on April 21, 1988, entitled "Drug Violence Undermining Queens Hopes," were the words, "[crack] violence is threatening the very stability of what has long been considered New York's most middle-class borough." A January 23, 1989 article in *New York Magazine* called "Fighting Back Against Crime" noted that "most neighborhoods in the city by now have been forced to deal with crack or its foul by-products: if not crack houses and street dealers or users, then crackhead crimes such as purse snatchings, car breakins, burglaries, knife-point robberies, muggings, and murders" (Pooley 1989, 32). On September 17, 1989 an article in *Time* magazine called "The Decline of New York" included the following: "A growing sense of vulnerability has been deepened by the belief that deadly violence, once mostly confined to crime-ridden ghetto neighborhoods that the police once wrote off as free-fire zones, is now lashing out randomly at anyone, even in areas once considered relatively safe" (Attinger 1989, 38).

Crack-related violence never was as random as the media portrayal in the late 1980s (Brownstein 1991a). Official statistics and ethnographic reports showed "most drug-related violence was confined to people who, by choice or circumstance, lived in or near drug communities and neighborhoods" (Brownstein 1991a, 95). Rather, as Reinarman and Levine pointed out in their analysis of the political context of the crack phenomenon, drug scares have a life of their own that is realized independent of observable patterns or trends of drug use or trafficking (1989, 537). These scares can and do, however, serve a purpose in that they can be used in support of the interests of various claims-makers in the marketplace of social problems.

The Interests of the Media in the Story of Violence

As an industry, the news media are in business to maximize profits by selling stories, either in print or over air waves, and by selling advertising space. As a social institution, the function of the news media is to inform the public, and therefore to secure access to information that it is in the interest of the public to know. That is, the interests of the news media include selling stories and advertising space and maintaining working relationships with the individuals and organizations that are able to provide access to the information needed to write those stories.

When official violent crime statistics first rose and then fell in major U.S. cities, the news media told and sold the story. To attract readers and advertisers, they told it as a sensational story, emphasizing themes that were both engaging and alarming at the same time. They also told it in a way that would "not contradict the policies of officials on whom they depended for information" (Brownstein 1991a, 98). In doing so, they participated in the promotion of a drug scare that encouraged public support for the expansion of law enforcement and the contraction of civil liberties during a period of fiscal crisis, overcrowding of the criminal justice system, and legitimate questions about the extent to which violence was actually increasing and spreading.

This is not to say that the media were part of a conspiracy to implement a reactionary criminal justice agenda. But it does suggest that as a claims-maker in the marketplace of social problems, the media was part of a cooperative effort to define and construct the problem of criminal violence as serious and in need of immediate and drastic action. In addition, it suggests that the media worked collaboratively with political and law enforcement officials to tell the story in that way.

Epilogue

When he was trying to save his job as Mayor of New York, David Dinkins used the news media to make known to voters who might not have noticed that crime had begun to decline in New York City during his watch. On January 5, 1993, an article appeared on the first page of the first section of *The New York Times* called, "Defending Record, Dinkins Sees City as a Safer Place."

The 1,690 words of the article were mostly about the fiscal accomplishments of the Mayor, but the headline was about crime. Dinkins nonetheless lost to Giuliani.

Like his fellow Mayor in New York, Kurt Schmoke in Baltimore used the media to make the case during an election year that he was responsible for making his city a safer place, despite its unimpressive crime statistics. A June 15, 1995 front page article in *The Sun* of Baltimore by Peter Hermann called "Crime steals peace of mind of city residents, officials Schmoke making strides; perception of danger remains" devoted 2,187 words to explaining with numerous quotes what had happened to crime in the city during the years of the Mayor's tenure. Despite the words "Crime seems to be out of control," the article was favorable to the Mayor, including a quote from the State Secretary of the Department of Public Safety and Correctional Services saying, "If you want to know if he's done a good job, the answer is yes." Schmoke was re-elected.

7

Why Drug Traffickers, Government, Law Enforcement, and the Media Constructed a Violent Crime Wave

In 1965 under Executive Order Number 11236, the President of the United States, Lyndon Johnson, established the Commission on Law Enforcement and Administration of Justice to report back to him about crime, the people involved in it, and what can be done to reduce it. In its official report, the Commission concluded, "There has always been too much crime. Virtually every generation since the founding of the Nation and before has felt itself threatened by the spectre of rising crime and violence" (President's Commission 1968, 101). What the Commission said then about the fear of crime and violence holds true today for the generation that is living through the last decades of the twentieth century. But whether or not there is now, or ever was, "too much crime" is difficult to say. In fact, once it is acknowledged and recognized that crime is a social construction, it becomes difficult to say how much there really is, let alone how much is too much.

As crime waves in the U.S. go, the crime wave from 1980 to 1994 was nothing special. What was special and most interesting was the public response to the wave. It gives credibility to the conclusion Christopher Jencks reached when he raised the question of whether or not violent crime was rising during this period: "Few subjects inspire as much nonsense as violent crime" (Jencks 1991, 109). Why did a relatively modest crime wave in the late twentieth century produce such a profound reaction?

The Political and Cultural Context of the Violent Crime Wave

In the earlier chapters of this book I discussed how the violent crime wave of the last decades of the twentieth century was the product of the "interpretations, decisions, and actions" of government policy-makers, law enforcement officials, and the news media. In addition, I demonstrated the significance for this construction of the "invention" of crack cocaine and the spread of crack markets. However, to understand why this collaboration came to pass and why crack cocaine was so important, it is necessary to understand the political and cultural contexts in which the wave of violent crime occurred.

The Poltical Context. Government criminal justice policy-makers and law enforcement officials are typically under pressure from the public to appear tough on crime. This is most apparent at the end of the twentieth century, following the social disturbance of the anti-war and civil rights rebellions of the 1960s, the political disruption of the Watergate shenanigans of the 1970s, and the fiscal dislocation that resulted from the war efforts—hot and cold—of the 1960s and the 1970s. Reinarman and Levine observed that after the damage it suffered from Watergate, the Republican Party courted the fundamentalist and conservative New Right with its emphasis on individuals as the source rather than the victims of trouble (1989, 561). Similarly, they observed that the Democratic Party during this period became defensive and responded with its own hard line against individual offenders (Reinarman and Levine 1989, 563). In terms of criminal justice policy, Diana Gordon characterized this shift, which began in the 1970s, as a "justice juggernaut" (1990). She suggests that the juggernaut found and continues to find its support in the political affinity between the philosophical concern that offending individuals get their "just deserts" and the fiscal concern that the vast and growing national debt is out of control (1990, chapters 6-8).

Theoretically, the policies that Gordon calls the justice juggernaut were grounded in "a paradigm shift in criminal justice ideology from the 'soft' approach of rehabilitation to the 'hard' one of deterrence, retribution, and incapacitation" (Gordon 1990, 15). Practically, they manifested themselves in an enormous expansion of the criminal justice system. In New York State, for example, from 1980 to 1990, felony arrests increased by 61 percent, felony convictions from indictment by 168 percent, and sentences to prison for felony conviction by 192 percent.

The most notable expansion of the criminal justice system during the 1980s involved drug offenses. For example, in New York State from 1980 to 1990, the number of felony drug arrests increased by 370 percent, the number of drug felony convictions from indictment by 991 percent, and the number of sentences to prison for drug offenses by an astounding 1,151 percent. Clearly, drugs, and particularly crack, had political utility for the political proponents and executors of the justice juggernaut. As noted earlier, Reinarman and Levine wrote:

> . . . the spread of cocaine and crack was a godsend to the New Right. They used 'drugs' as an ideological fig leaf to place over the unsightly urban ills that had increased markedly under [President Ronald] Reagan administration social and fiscal policies. 'The drug problem' served as an all-purpose scapegoat with which they could blame an array of problems on the deviance of the individuals who suffered them. (Reinarman and Levine 1989, 561-62)

The Cultural Context. On June 14, 1996, the headline of the *New York Post* read in large bold letters: "ONE-MAN CRIME WAVE." The police had arrested one man who was believed to have been responsible for four particularly violent crimes. Pages one through five of the newspaper were devoted to the story with headlines such as the following: "One Bust Solves Four Crimes," "He finally pours out grisly truth after 6 hrs.," City Breathes Easier, But the Anger Lingers," and "Rudy has everything to fear from fear itself." The last one, on page 4, caught my attention.

Under the last heading, in an article marked "Analysis," the City Hall Bureau Chief for *The Post* wrote, "Mayor Giuliani has demonstrated an ability to manage city government, the fragile city budget and the public agenda. But now he has a much tougher management assignment on his hands—the management of fear" (Seifman 1996, 4). The point of the article was that despite the remarkable decline in both the violent crime rate in the city and the low crime ranking of New York among cities, the reputation of the city as safe was very fragile. A few violent crimes against strangers, a little public panic, and all is lost. As the article said, "Disney isn't interested in pouring millions into a city where crime is an overriding issue. Tourists will flee at the mere hint of random violence" (Seifman 1996, 4).

In terms of public safety, the signs and symbols of crime are at least as important at the actual rate of criminal offending. In a recently published book, Jeff Ferrell and Clint Sanders argue for a "cultural criminology" (1995). They suggest that "there is a common ground between cultural and criminal practices in contemporary social life—that is, between collective behavior organized around imagery, style, and symbolic meaning, and that categorized by legal and political authorities as criminal" (1995, 3). Their conception of cultural criminology is a useful context for understanding the social construction of a violent crime wave near the end of the twentieth century in the United States.

Inherent in the notion of social constructionism is the acknowledgment that culturally defined symbols and images are integrally related to socially defined projects and programs. In terms of the observed rise and fall of violent crime in the United States from the early 1980s to the middle of the 1990s, this relationship is made clear in the way the interests of government, law enforcement, and the media contributed to the symbolic construction of a violent crime wave that resulted in the creation and implementation of programs and policies in support of those interests.

This is *not* to say that the wave of violent crime had no basis in reality, nor that there was a baneful conspiracy to make the public believe that violent crime was either rising or falling. Government policy-makers, law enforcement officials, and media reporters are not that well organized and not that concerned with the interests of others to conspire or even formally collaborate to deceive the public. Nonetheless, by acting in their own political and economic interests, these powerful social institutions did use the resources and symbols at their disposal both to define the parameters of the social problem of violence and to produce an authoritative measure of that violence that convinced the public of the need for extreme action.

The Social Construction of Violent Crime

The notion of conspiracy brings to mind secret meetings and memos and evil intentions and purposes. There is no reason to believe that any institution or individual was involved in any evil or secret scheme to deceive the public about crack cocaine or the extent to which violence was associated with it. Yet it is clear that at different times and under different circumstances it is in the common interest of government, law enforcement, and the media to mutually present a particular image of violent crime to the public. Such was the case when crack cocaine came on the scene in the 1980s. Social constructionism provides a valuable perspective for understanding how and why this happened. As Gordon wrote, "Viewing crime as a political and social construct makes it easier to see criminal justice policy shaped by forces more fundamental than crime rates or victimization—or even the intense political contest that exploits the fear of crime" (1990, 153).

Social constructionism has two aspects, the *definition* and the *production* of social phenomena. Social phenomena are *defined* through the social processes that identify or give meaning to them, such as interpretation, claims-making, or labeling. Social phenomena are *produced* through their realization or actualization in the decisions and actions or interactions of individuals. The problem of violence, specifically crack-related violence, in the United States near the end of the twentieth century was both socially defined and socially produced. It was socially defined through the claims and interpretations of criminal justice policy-makers, law enforcement officials, and the news media. It was socially produced through the decisions and actions of the individuals working in and for those institutions.

Public Policy and the Public Interest

Because they occur in a political context, criminal justice policy and practice are inevitably oriented to the short term (Brownstein and Goldstein 1990). Decisions, interpretations, and actions are made or taken in relation to recurring political cycles, such as the preparation of annual administrative budgets or the procession of periodic civic elections, or in response to real or perceived crises invariably demanding immediate attention and response. In this context it is difficult if not impossible to propose policies or implement programs and practices that require time and resources to bear results, such as crime prevention or drug treatment programs, or job training or educational programs. The results have to be visible by the next election, or by the time the next round of budget decisions are made. Consequently, those policies and practices that are easily interpreted as successful or can symbolically be defined as successful are most favored by public policy-makers and officials. They are also the ones most readily rewarded by the media.

In the early 1980s, criminal justice policy-makers were under pressure to get tough on crime while finding ways to reduce government spending. Law enforcement officials likewise had to get tough on crime, their constraint being that they had to do so with limited or reduced resources. Crack proved useful to them both.

Following their emergence in U.S. cities, crack markets followed an economic cycle of growth, expansion, and stabilization. As a newly opened market for a new and lucrative product grew and expanded, competition was fierce among young entrepreneurs with little or no business experience and few if any links to legitimate or even illegitimate institutions or enterprises. These business operators freely competed with each other, commonly using violence to resolve conflicts or disputes over money or market share. As the market stabilized, competition and along with it violence diminished. In terms of the official record of violence in the U.S. during this period, it would appear that the high level of violence, including lethal violence, of the late 1980s was in fact as much symbolic as it was real.

Crack provided a symbol around which policies and practices could be constructed. With a demon as dangerous as crack, fiscal restraints could not be allowed to stand in the way of tough policies and practices. Plus, crack provided a symbol that could be used to label a category of criminal offenses and offenders as particularly heinous, and thereby facilitated the measurement of progress in the short term; whether or not crime decreases or social life in a community improves, more arrests and more prosecutions of crack fiends provided a simple measure of what the public deemed a good and positive result. Consequently, crack served as a symbol for the construction of mechanisms for passing federal dollars to state and local criminal justice and law enforcement agencies.

Crack served the needs of the news media as well. Not only was rising violence a good story to tell and sell, the overwhelming criminal justice response to crack was itself a good story. However, to gain access to that story, the media needed to have access to government policy-makers and law enforcement officials who would share the story with them.

Simply, in the political context of short-term decision-making and action, crack cocaine provided a powerful symbol for government policy-makers, law enforcement officials, and the news media to work together in their own and mutual interests. Ultimately, they lost sight of their responsibility to serve the public interest and focused instead on their own political and economic interests.

Reinarman and Levine ask "what's the harm in a little hysteria?" (1989, 567). In this case, the harm is that the attention to the constructed and symbolic violence of the crack market expansion era took attention and resources from the social structural problems that give rise to violence in the long term—poverty, inadequate education and health care, homelessness, corporate and environmental pollution, employee wage exploitation, and so on. The response to crack-related violence drew attention from the real problems. The public could be convinced that government and law enforcement were doing something to help the community, even if in fact they were not. It took money from programs where it was needed and could have done something—though those areas are longer term issues and to see a positive result would take more than a single budget or election cycle.

Conclusion

When he originally wrote *The Rules of Sociological Method* at the end of the nineteenth century, Emile Durkheim observed that crime is normal. As later translated to English, he wrote:

> In the first place crime is normal because a society exempt
> from it is utterly impossible. Crime . . . consists of an act that
> offends certain very strong collective sentiments. In a society
> in which criminal acts are no longer committed, the
> sentiments they offend would have to be found to exist with
> the same degree as sentiments contrary to them. Assuming
> that this condition could actually be realized, crime would
> not thereby disappear; it would only change its form, for the
> very cause which would thus dry up the sources of
> criminality would immediately open up new ones. (1938, 67)

That is, a society without crime cannot exist. Crime is inevitable.

Given that crime is inevitable in any given society, the level of crime in a society cannot be expected to ceaselessly fall until crime is no more. Rather, the level of crime in a society can only rise and fall, surging and billowing forward through time in a rhythm of more or less crime. Therefore, the current decline in the level of crime in the United States inevitably will come to an end. Ultimately it will be followed by a period of rising crime, to be followed in turn by a period of declining crime. Thus the wave of crime that has been observed at the end of the twentieth century undoubtedly will be followed by a crime wave of some unknown measure early in the twenty-first.

Any number of social forces can provide the impetus for a change in the level of crime in society. In the U.S. at the tail end of the twentieth century or the first years of the twenty-first, the rise may come in response to changing patterns of drug use and trade, perhaps being driven by the resurgence of heroin being reported by the Office of National Drug Control Policy. Many criminologists believe it will be driven by demographics, by an increased number of young people and the alarming proclivity of contemporary young people to engage in violence (Blumstein 1996; Snyder and Sickmund 1995; Snyder, Sickmund, and Poe-Yamagata 1996).

While it is certain that the level of crime will fluctuate, the extent to which it will rise and fall is more difficult to foretell. Of greater concern to us as citizens of a free and democratic society, however, is the manner in which we respond to future crime waves. Starting from the fiscal and social conservatism with which the current violent crime wave has thoroughly drenched us, a similar reaction to the next wave by us and our social representatives—government policy-makers, law enforcement officials, and the news media—could dramatically alter the character of our society.

There are two things we need to consider. First, we are

forewarned. We know that a crime wave, probably violent, is inevitable in the U.S. in the early years of the twenty-first century. We do not know how high it will rise before it falls, but we know that for some period of time and in some measure it will increase the level of crime. Instead of sounding the alarm, however, we should use the opportunity to prepare. For example, we know that in the near future there will be more young people and that young people account for much of our crime, increasingly our violent crime. We need now to think about ways to prevent young people from becoming involved in crime. We cannot stop all crime from happening or all young people from participating in it, but perhaps we can identify programs that work, such as building places and planning activities for young people besides *chillin' on the corner or hangin' out at the mall*. And we can invest in the social infrastructure—including our educational systems, our job training programs, and employment opportunities—that provide young people with realistic alternatives to criminal activity.

Second, we need to encourage our public representatives to be more responsible in the ways they interpret and use the inevitable changes in the level of crime as measured and observed, officially or otherwise. As citizens, we need to avoid hysteria. As public officials, government policy-makers, law enforcement officials, and the news media need to devote more resources and effort to understanding and explaining the measures. That is, we need to encourage them and they need to act in the public interest.

References

ALBERT (COHEN), M. 1986. *Criminal Possession of Controlled Substances: Analysis of Criminal Justice Processing*. Albany, NY: Division of Criminal Justice Services.

ALBERT (COHEN), M. and T. HARIG 1986. *Criminal Sales of Controlled Substances: Analysis of Criminal Justice Processing*. Albany, NY: Division of Criminal Justice Services.

ANTI-DRUG ABUSE COUNCIL. 1990. *State of New York Anti-Drug Abuse Strategy Report*. Albany, NY: Statewide Anti-Drug Abuse Council.

ANTI-DRUG ABUSE COUNCIL. 1989. *State of New York Anti-Drug Abuse Strategy Report*. Albany, NY: Statewide Anti-Drug Abuse Council.

ARENDT, H. 1969. *On Violence*. New York: Harcourt, Brace & World, Inc.

ATTINGER, J. 1989. "The Decline of New York." *Time* September

17:36-41,44.

BAKALAR, J.B. and L. GRINSPOON. 1984. *Drug Control in a Free Society.* Cambridge: Cambridge University Press.

BARAK, G. 1988. "Newsmaking Criminology: Reflections on the Media, Intellectuals, and Crime." *Justice Quarterly* 5:565-87.

BARNETT, A. 1988."Drug Crackdowns and Crime Rates: A Comment on the Kleiman Report." Pp. 35-42 in M.R. Chaiken (ed.), *Street-Level Drug Enforcement: Examining the Issues.* Issues and Practices. Washington, D.C.: National Institute of Justice.

BEALS, G. and E. THOMAS. 1996. "A Crimebuster's Fall." *Newsweek.* April 8:42.

BELENKO, S. 1990. "The Impact of Drug Offenders on the Criminal Justice System." Pp. 27-48 in R.A. Weisheit, ed., *Drugs, Crime and the Criminal Justice System.* Cincinnati: Anderson.

BERGER, P.L. 1963. *Invitation to Sociology: A Humanistic Perspective.* Garden City, NY: Anchor Books.

BERGER, P.L. and T. LUCKMANN. 1966. *The Social Construction of Reality—A Treatise in the Sociology of Knowledge.* Garden City, NY: Doubleday and Company, Inc.

BEST, J. 1993. "But Seriously Folks: The Limitations of the Strict Constructionist Interpretation of Social Problems." Pp. 109-27 in G. Miller and J.A. Holstein, eds., *Constructionist Controversies—Issues in Social Problems Theory.* New York: Aldine de Gruyter.

BEST, J. 1990. *Threatened Children—Rhetoric and Concern about Child-Victims.* Chicago: University of Chicago Press.

BEST, J. 1989. *Images of Issues: Typifying Contemporary Social Problems.* New York: Aldine de Gruyter.

BLUMSTEIN, A. 1996. "Youth Violence, Guns, and Illicit Drug Markets." *National Institute of Justice Research Preview.*

Washington, D.C.: U.S. Department of Justice.

BLUMSTEIN, A.1995. "Violence by Young People: Why the Deadly Nexus?" Pp. 2-9 in *National Institute of Justice Journal*. Washington, D.C.: U.S. Department of Justice.

BLUMSTEIN, A., J. COHEN, and R. ROSENFELD. 1992. "The UCR-NCS Relationship Revisited: A Reply to Menard." *Criminology* 30:115-24.

BLUMSTEIN, A., J. COHEN, and R. ROSENFELD. 1991. "Trend and Deviation in Crime Rates: A Comparison of UCR and NCS data for Burglary and Robbery." *Criminology* 29:237-63.

BOURGOIS, P. 1995. *In Search of Respect—Selling Crack in El Barrio*. Cambridge: Cambridge University Press.

BOUZA, A.V. 1988. "Evaluating Street-Level Drug Enforcement." Pp. 43-48 in M.R. Chaiken, (ed.), *Street-Level Drug Enforcement: Examining the Issues*. Issues and Practices. Washington, D.C.: National Institute of Justice.

BROWNSTEIN, H.H. 1995. "The Social Construction of Crime Problems: Insiders and the Use of Official Statistics."*Journal of Crime and Justice* 18:17-30.

BROWNSTEIN, H.H.1992. "Making Peace in the War on Drugs." *Humanity and Society* 16:217-35.

BROWNSTEIN, H.H.1991a. "The Media and the Construction of Random Drug Violence." *Social Justice* 18:85-103.

BROWNSTEIN, H.H.1991b. "The Social Construction of Public Policy: A Case for Participation by Researchers." *Sociological Practice Review* 2:132-40.

BROWNSTEIN, H.H., H.R.S. BAXI, P.J. GOLDSTEIN, and P.J. RYAN. 1992. "The Relationship of Drugs, Drug Trafficking, and Drug Traffickers to Homicide." *Journal of Crime and Justice* 15: 25-44.

BROWNSTEIN, H.H. and P.J. GOLDSTEIN. 1990. "Research and the Development of Public Policy: The Case of Drugs and

Violent Crime." *Journal of Applied Sociology* 7:77-92

BUREAU OF JUSTICE STATISTICS. 1994. *Criminal Victimization in the United States: 1973-92 Trends*. Washington, D.C.: U.S. Department of Justice.

BUREAU OF JUSTICE STATISTICS. 1988. *Report to the Nation on Crime and Justice.* 2nd Edition. NCJ-105506. Washington, D.C.: U.S. Department of Justice.

CHAIKEN, M.R. 1988. *Street-Level Drug Enforcement: Examining the Issues*. Issues and Practices. Washington, D.C.: National Institute of Justice.

CONSTANTINE, T.A. 1992. *New York State Police Assessment of Drug, Gang, and Violent Crime Activity in Upstate New York*. Albany, NY: New York State Police.

CUOMO, M. 1989. *Message to the Legislature*. January 4. Albany, New York.

CUOMO, M. 1987. *Message to the Legislature*. January 7. Albany, New York.

DIVISION OF CRIMINAL JUSTICE SERVICES. 1995. *Crime and Justice Annual Report, 1994*. Albany, NY: New York State Division of Criminal Justice Services.

DIVISION OF CRIMINAL JUSTICE SERVICES. 1988. *Crime and Justice Annual Report, 1987*. Albany, NY: New York State Division of Criminal Justice Services.

DIVISION OF CRIMINAL JUSTICE SERVICES. 1977. *New York State—Uniform Crime Reporting Procedures*. Albany, NY: New York State Division of Criminal Justice Services.

DIVISION OF SUBSTANCE ABUSE SERVICES. 1986. *A Study of Crack Smokers*. Albany, NY: Division of Substance Abuse Services.

DUNWORTH, T. and A. SAIGER. 1994. "Drugs and Crime in Public Housing: A Three-City Analysis." *National Institute of Justice Research Report*. Washington, D.C.: U.S. Department of Justice.

DURKHEIM, E. 1938. *The Rules of Sociological Method*. Eighth edition, Tr. by S.A. Solovay and J.H. Mueller and edited by G.E.G. Catlin. New York: The Free Press.

DUSTER, T. 1970. *The Legislation of Morality*. New York: Free Press.

ECK, J.E. and L.J. RICCIO. "Relationship Between Reported Crime Rates and Victimization Survey Results: An Empirical and Analytic Study." *Journal of Criminal Justice* 7:293-308.

FAGAN, J. and K. CHIN. 1990. "Violence as Regulation and Social Control in the Distribution of Crack." Pp. 8-43 in M. De La Rosa, E.Y. Lambert, and B. Gropper, eds., *Drugs and Violence: Causes, Correlates, and Consequences*. Washington, D.C.: National Institute on Drug Abuse.

FALCO, M.1989. *Winning the Drug War: A National Strategy*. New York: Priority Press.

FEDERAL BUREAU OF INVESTIGATION. 1995. *Crime in the United States, 1994*. Washington, D.C.: U.S. Department of Justice.

FEDERAL BUREAU OF INVESTIGATION.1994. *Crime in the United States, 1993*. Washington, D.C.: U.S. Department of Justice.

FEDERAL BUREAU OF INVESTIGATION.1993. *Crime in the United States, 1992*. Washington, D.C.: U.S. Department of Justice.

FERRELL, J. and C.R. SANDERS. 1995. *Cultural Criminology*. Boston: Northeastern University Press.

GERTH, H.H. and C.W. MILLS. 1946. *From Max Weber: Essays in Sociology*. New York: Oxford University Press.

GOLDSTEIN, H. 1993. "The New Policing: Confronting Complexity." *National Institute of Justice Research in Brief*. Washington, D.C.: U.S. Department of Justice.

GOLDSTEIN, P.J., H.H. BROWNSTEIN, and P.J. RYAN. 1992. "Drug-Related Homicide in New York: 1984 and 1988."

Crime and Delinquency 38: 459-76.

GOLDSTEIN, P.J., H.H. BROWNSTEIN, P.J. RYAN, and P.A. BELLUCCI. 1989. "Crack and Homicide in New York City, 1988: A Conceptually Based Event Analysis." *Contemporary Drug Problems*. Winter: 651-87.

GORDON, D.R. 1990. *The Justice Juggernaut: Fighting Street Crime, Controlling Citizens*. New Brunswick: Rutgers University Press.

GOVE, W., M. HUGHES, and M. GEERKEN. 1985. "Are Uniform Crime Reports a Valid Indicator of the Index Crime? An Affirmative Answer With Minor Qualifications." *Criminology* 23:234-37.

GOVERNOR'S OFFICE OF EMPLOYEE RELATIONS. 1986a. "Crackdown on crack." *GOER News*. Albany, New York. August: Governor's Page.

GOVERNOR'S OFFICE OF EMPLOYEE RELATIONS.1986b. "Crack—The Deadliest Cocaine of All." *GOER News*. Albany, New York. September:11-12.

GREENBERG, J. 1990. "All About Crime." *New York Magazine* 23:20-32.

HAYESLIP, J.R., D.W. 1989. "Local-level Drug Enforcement: New Strategies." Pp. 2-7 in *NIJ Reports, Research in Action* March/April no. 213. Washington, D.C. National Institute of Justice.

HAZELRIGG, L.E. 1985. "Were It Not For Words." *Social Problems* 32:234-37.

HILLSMAN, S.T., S. SADD, M.L. SULLIVAN, M. SVIRIDOFF. 1989. *The Community Effects of Street Level Narcotics Enforcement: A Study of the New York City Police Department's Tactical Narcotics Teams*. New York: Vera Institute of Justice.

HINDELANG, M.J., T. HIRSCHI, and J.G. WEIS. 1979. "Correlates of Delinquency: The Illusion of Discrepancy Between Self-Report and Official Measures." *American Sociological*

Review 44:995-1014.

INCIARDI, J.A. 1992. *The War on Drugs II—The Continuing Epic of Heroin, Cocaine, Crack, Crime, AIDS, and Public Policy.* Mountain View, CA: Mayfield Publishing Company.

INCIARDI, J.A.1989. "Beyond Cocaine: Basuco, Crack, and Other Coca Products." *Contemporary Drug Problems* 14:461-92.

INCIARDI, J.A., D. LOCKWOOD, AND A.E. POTTIEGER. 1993. *Women and Crack-Cocaine.* New York: MacMillan Publishing Company.

JENCKS, C. 1991. "Behind the Numbers—Is Violent Crime Increasing?" *The American Prospect* Winter:98-109.

JENKINS, P. 1994a. "The 'Ice Age'—The Social Construction of a Drug Panic." *Justice Quarterly* 11:7-31.

JENKINS, P.1994b. *Using Murder—The Social Construction of Serial Homicide.* New York: Aldine de Gruyter.

JENSEN, G.F. and M. KARPOS. 1993. "Managing Rape: Exploratory Research on the Behavior of Rape Statistics." *Criminology* 31:363-85.

JOHNSON, B.D., A. GOLUB, and J. FAGAN. 1995. "Careers in Crack, Drug Use, Drug Distribution, and Nondrug Criminality." *Crime and Delinquency* 41:275-95.

JOHNSON, B.D., A. HAMID, and H. SANABRIA. 1992. "Emerging Models of Crack Distribution." Pp. 56-78 in T. Mieczkowski, ed., *Drugs, Crime, and Social Policy: Research, Issues, and Concerns.* Boston: Allyn and Bacon.

JORDAN, G.E. and M. GELMAN. 1990. "Officials Talk of Cutting TNT." *Newsday* May 4:7,29.

KAPLAN, J. 1970. *Marijuana—The New Prohibition.* New York: The World Publishing Company.

KITSUSE, J.I. and A.V. CICOUREL. 1963. "A Note on the Uses of Official Statistics." *Social Problems* 11:131-39.

KLEIMAN, M.A.R. 1988. "Crackdowns. The Effects of Intensive Enforcement on Retail Heroin Dealing." Pp. 3-34 in M.R.

Chaiken, ed., *Street-Level Drug Enforcement: Examining the Issues. Issues and Practices.* Washington, D.C.: National Institute of Justice.

KLEIN, M.W. and C.L. MAXSON. 1994. "Gangs and Crack Cocaine Trafficking." Pp. 42-58 in D.L. MacKenzie and C.D. Uchida, eds., *Drugs and Crime—Evaluating Public Policy Initiatives.* Thousand Oaks: Sage Publications.

KOCH, T. 1990. *The News as Myth—Fact and Context in Journalism.* New York: Greenwood Press.

KRATCOSKI, P.C. and D. DUKES. 1995. "Perspectives on Community Policing." Pp. 5-20 in P.C. Kratcoski and D. Dukes, eds., *Issues in Community Policing.* Cincinnati: Anderson Publishing Company.

KRAUSS, C. 1996. "Police to Start Big Offensive Against Drugs." The New York Times. April 4:B1,B4.

LEE, A.M. 1978. *Sociology for Whom?* New York: Oxford University Press.

LEE, A.M. 1973. *The Daily Newspaper in America—The Evolution of a Social Instrument.* New York: Octagon Books.

LEE, A.M. and E.B. LEE. 1939. *The Fine Art of Propaganda—A Study of Father Coughlin's Speeches.* New York: Harcourt, Brace and Company.

MAHONEY, J. 1993. "Residents Cheer Massive Drug Raid." *Albany Times Union.* November: A1, A11.

MAHONEY, J. 1992. "NYC Drug Gangs Blamed for Rise in Upstate Crime." *Albany Times Union.* November:A1,A8.

MALTZ, M.D. 1975. "Crime Statistics: A Mathematical Perspective." *Journal of Criminal Justice* 3:177-94.

MASSING, M. 1989. "Crack's Destructive Sprint Across America." *New York Times Magazine* October 1: 38,40-1,58,60,62.

MASTROFSKI, S.D. and J.R. GREENE. 1993. "Community Policing and the Rule of Law." Pp. 80-102 in D. Weisburd and C. Uchida, eds., *Police Innovation and Control of the Police.*

New York: Springer-Verlag.

MASTROFSKI, S.D., R.E. WORDEN, and J.B. SNIPES. 1995. "Law Enforcement in a Time of Community Policing." *Criminology* 33:539-63.

MAYER, M. 1987. *Making News*. Garden City, NY: Doubleday and Company.

MCCARTHY, J.D., C. MCPHAIL, and J. SMITH. 1996. "Images of Protest: Dimensions of Selection Bias in Media Coverage of Washington Demonstrations, 1982 and 1991." *American Sociological Review* 61:478-99.

MCDOWALL, D. AND C. LOFTIN. 1992. "Comparing the UCR and NCS Over Time." *Criminology* 30:125-32.

MCELROY, J.E., C.A. COSGROVE, and S. SADD. 1993. *Community Policing—The CPOP in New York*. Newbury Park: Sage Publications.

MCGLONE, T. 1993. "Drug Raid Rounds Up Suspects." *Schenectady Daily Gazette*. November:A1, A4.

MENARD, S. 1992. "Residual Gains, Reliability, and the UCR-NCS Relationship: A Comment on Blumstein, Cohen, and Rosenfeld." *Criminology* 30:105-113.

MENARD, S. 1991. "Encouraging News for Criminologists (In the Year 2050)?" A Comment on O'Brien." *Journal of Criminal Justice* 19:563-67.

MENARD, S. and H.C. COVEY. 1988. "UCR and NCS: Comparison Over Space and Time." *Journal of Criminal Justice* 16:371-84.

MIECZKOWSKI, T. 1990. "Crack Distribution in Detroit." *Contemporary Drug Problems* 17:9-29.

MILLER, G. and J.A. HOLSTEIN. 1993. "Constructing Social Problems: Context and Legacy." Pp. 3-18 in G. Miller and J.A. Holstein, eds., *Constructionist Controversies—Issues in Social Problems Theory*. New York: Aldine de Gruyter.

MOORE, M.H. 1977. *Buy and Bust—The Effective Regulation of* an *Illicit Market in Heroin*. Lexington, MA: Lexington Books.

MOORE, M.H. and M.A.R. KLEIMAN. 1989. "The Police and Drugs." *Perspectives on Policing*, September, no. 11. Washington, D.C.: National Institute of Justice.

MUSTO, D.F. 1973. *The American Disease*. New Haven: Yale University Press.

NATIONAL COMMISSION ON THE CAUSES AND PREVENTION OF VIOLENCE. 1969.*To Establish Justice and Ensure Domestic Tranquility*. Washington, D.C.: Government Printing Office.

NEWMAN, G. 1979. *Understanding Violence*. New York: J.B. Lippincott Company.

O'BRIEN, R.M. 1996. "Police Productivity and Crime Rates: 1973-1992." *Criminology* 34:183-207.

O'BRIEN, R.M.1991. "Detrended UCR and NCS Crime Rates: Their Utility and Meaning." *Journal of Criminal Justice* 19:569-74.

O'BRIEN, R.M.1990. "Comparing Detrended UCR and NCS Crime Rates Over Time: 1973-1986." *Journal of Criminal Justice* 16:229-38.

OFFICE OF NATIONAL DRUG CONTROL POLICY. 1990. *National Drug Control Strategy*. Washington, D.C.: The White House.

OFFICE OF NATIONAL DRUG CONTROL POLICY.1989. *National Drug Control Strategy*. Washington, D.C.: The White House.

OFFICE OF THE ATTORNEY GENERAL. 1989. *Drug Trafficking—A Report to the President of the United States*. Washington, D.C.: U.S. Department of Justice.

PERKINS, C. AND P. KLAUS. 1996. "Criminal Victimization 1994." *Bureau of Justice Statistics Bulletin*. Washington, D.C.: U.S. Department of Justice.

PFOHL, S. 1985. "Toward a Sociological Deconstruction of Social Problems." *Social Problems* 32:228-32.

POLLNER, M. 1993. "The Reflexivity of Constructionism and the Construction of Reflexivity." Pp. 69-82 in G. Miller and J.A. Holstein, eds., *Constructionist Controversies—Issues in Social Problems Theory*. New York: Aldine de Gruyter.

POOLEY, E. 1996. "Police Commissioner William Bratton Set Out To Prove that Cops Really Can Cut Crime." *Time* 147:54-56.

PRESIDENT'S COMMISSION ON LAW ENFORCEMENT AND ADMINISTRATION OF JUSTICE. 1968. *The Challenge of Crime in a Free Society*. New York: Avon Books.

QUINNEY, R. and J. WILDEMAN. 1977. *The Problem of Crime— A Critical Introduction to Criminology*. New York: Harper and Row.

RAFTER, N.H. 1992a. "Claims-Making and Socio-Cultural Context in the First U.S. Eugenics Campaign." *Social Problems* 39:17-34.

RAFTER, N.H. 1992b. "Some Consequences of Strict Constructionism." *Social Problems* 39:38-39.

RAFTER, N.H. 1990. "The Social Construction of Crime and Crime Control." *Journal of Research in Crime and Delinquency* 27:376-89.

REINARMAN, C. and H.G. LEVINE. 1989. "Crack in Context: Politics and Media in the Making of a Drug Scare." *Contemporary Drug Problems* 16:535-77.

REUTER, P. 1991. "On the Consequences of Toughness." *A RAND Note* N-3447-DPRC:138-164.

REUTER, P., R. MACCOUN, and P. MURPHY. 1990. *Money From Crime: A Study of the Economics of Drug Dealing in Washington, D.C.* Santa Monica: RAND.

ROSS, J.I. 1995. "Confronting Community Policing: Minimizing Community Policing as Public Relations." Pp. 243-59 in P.C. Kratcoski and D. Dukes, eds., *Issues in Community Policing*.

Cincinnati: Anderson Publishing Company.

ROSS, R. and M. COHEN. 1988. *New York Trends in Felony Drug Offense Processing*. Albany, NY: New York State Division of Criminal Justice Services.

ROTH, J.A. 1994a. "Firearms and Violence." *National Institute of Justice Research in Brief*. Washington, D.C.: U.S. Department of Justice.

ROTH, J.A.1994b. "Understanding and Preventing Violence." *National Institute of Justice Research in Brief*. Washington, D.C.: U.S. Department of Justice.

SCHNEIDER, J.W. 1985. "Defining the Definitional Perspective on Social Problems." *Social Problems* 32:232-34.

SCHUTZ, A. 1962. *Collected Papers I. The Problem of Social Reality*. Edited with an Introduction by M. Natanson. The Hague: Martinus Nijhoff.

SEIFMAN, D. 1996. "Rudy has everything to fear from fear itself." *New York Post* June 14:4.

SENATE JUDICIARY COMMITTEE. 1990. *Fighting Drug Abuse: A National Strategy*, January. Washington, D.C.: U.S. Senate.

SHAPIRO, BRUCE. 1996. "How the War on Crime Imprisons America." *The Nation* 262:14-21.

SHERMAN, L.W. 1990. "Police Crackdowns." *NIJ Reports, Research in Action*. March/April, no. 219. Washington, D.C.: National Institute of Justice.

SHERMAN, L.W., D.P. ROGAN, and OTHERS. 1995. "Deterrent Effects of Police Raids on Crack Houses: A Randomized, Controlled, Experiment." *Justice Quarterly* 12:755-81.

SKOGAN, W. 1974. "The Validity of Official Crime Statistics: An Empirical Investigation." *Social Science Quarterly* 55:25-38.

SKOLNICK, J.H. 1966. *Justice Without Trial—Law Enforcement in Democratic Society*. New York: John Wiley and Sons, Inc.

SKOLNICK, J.H. and D.H. BAYLEY. 1988. "Community Policing: Issues and Practices Around the World." *National Insti-*

tute of Justice Issues and Practices. Washington, D.C.: U.S. Department of Justice.

SMITH, M.E., M. SVIRIDOFF, S. SADD, R. CURTIS, and R. GRINC. 1992. *The Neighborhood Effects of Street-Level Drug Enforcement—Tactical Narcotics Teams in New York— An Evaluation of TNT.* New York: The Vera Institute of Justice.

SNYDER, H.N. and M. SICKMUND. 1995. *Juvenile Offenders and Victims: A National Report.* Office of Juvenile Justice and Delinquency Prevention. Washington, D.C.: U.S. Department of Justice.

SNYDER, H.N., M. SICKMUND, and E. POE-YAMAGATA. 1996. *Juvenile Offenders and Victims: 1996 Update on Violence.* Office of Juvenile Justice and Delinquency Prevention. Washington, D.C.: U.S. Department of Justice.

SOREL, G. 1950. *Reflections on Violence.* Tr. by T.E. Hulme and J. Roth. Glencoe: The Free Press.

SPECTOR, M. AND J.I. KITSUSE. 1974. "Social Problems: A Re-Formulation." *Social Problems* 21:145-59.

SPECTOR, M. AND J.I. KITSUSE. 1987. *Constructing Social Problems.* New York: Aldine de Gruyter.

STARR, P. 1987. "The Sociology of Official Statistics." Pp. 7-57 in W. Alonso and P. Starr, eds., *The Politics of Numbers.* New York: Russell Sage Foundation.

STIGLIANO, T. 1983. "Jean-Paul Sartre on Understanding Violence." *Crime and Social Justice* 19:52-64.

SVIRIDOFF, M. and S.T. HILLSMAN. 1994. "Assessing the Community Effects of Tactical Narcotics Teams." Pp. 114-28 in D.L. MacKenzie and C.D. Uchida, eds., *Drugs and Crime— Evaluating Public Policy Initiatives.* Thousand Oaks: Sage Publications.

TASK FORCE ON THE POLICE. 1967. *Task Force Report: The Police.* Washington, D.C.: The President's Commission on

Law Enforcement and Administration of Justice.

THORNBERRY, T.P. AND M. FARNWORTH. 1982. "Social Correlates of Criminal Involvement: Further Evidence of the Relations Between Social Status and Criminal Behavior." *American Sociological Review* 47:505-18.

TREBACH, A.S. 1982. *The Heroin Solution.* New Haven: Yale University Press.

TROJANOWICZ, R. and B. BUCQUEROUX. 1990. *Community Policing—A Contemporary Perspective.* Cincinnati: Anderson Publishing Company.

TROYER, R.J. 1992. "Some Consequences of Contextual Constructionism." *Social Problems* 39:35-37.

WEBER, M. 1947. *The Theory of Social and Economic Organization.* Tr. by A.M. Henderson and T. Parsons and edited with an Introduction by T. Parsons. New York: The Free Press.

WEINER, N.A. and M.E. WOLFGANG. 1985. "The Extent and Character of Violent Crime in America, 1969 to 1982." Pp. 17-39 in L.A. Curtis, ed., *American Violence and Public Policy.* New Haven: Yale University Press.

WEINGART, S.N., F.X. HARTMAN, and D. OSBORNE. 1994. "Case Studies of Community Anti-Drug Efforts." *National Institute of Justice Research in Brief.* Washington, D.C.: U.S. Department of Justice.

WEISHEIT, R.A. 1990. "Civil War on Drugs." Pp. 1-10 in R.A. Weisheit, ed., *Drugs, Crime and the Criminal Justice System.* Cincinnati: Anderson.

WILLIAMS, T. 1992. *Crackhouse—Notes from the End of the Line.* New York: Penguin Books.

WILLIAMS, T.1989. *Cocaine Kids—The Inside Story of a Teenage Drug Ring.* Reading, MA: Addison-Wesley Publishing Company, Inc.

WILSON, J.Q. 1971. *Varieties of Police Behavior: The Management of Law and Order in Eight Communities.* New York:

Atheneum.

WILSON, J.Q. and G.L. KELLING. 1982. "The Police and Neighborhood Safety—Broken Windows." *The Atlantic Monthly* 249:29-38.

WISOTSKY, S. 1986. *Breaking the Impasse in the War on Drugs*. New York: Greenwood Press.

WITKIN, G. 1991. "The Men Who Created Crack." *U.S. News and World Report* August: 44-53.

WOOLGAR, S. and D. PAWLUCH. 1985a. "Ontological Gerrymandering: The Anatomy of Social Problems Explanations." *Social Problems* 32:214-227.

WOOLGAR, S. and D. PAWLUCH. 1985b. "How Shall We Move Beyond Constructivism?" *Social Problems* 33:159-62.

ZIMMER, L. 1987. "Operation Pressure Point: The Disruption of Street-Level Drug Trade on New York's Lower East Side." Occasional Papers from the Center for Research in Crime and Justice, New York University School of Law.

Index

Close Control: Managing a Maximum Security Prison
The Story of Ragen's Stateville Penitentiary

by **Nathan Kantrowitz**

IN A FEW WORDS: This has to be the most interesting and provocative book on prisons for many a decade. Not only is it a fascinating account of why firm prison control is needed, and how it works, but it is a history, of sorts, of how Warden Ragen controlled the Stateville-Joliet prison back in the 1960's. In fact, the original manuscript of this book was written by Kantrowitz when he was the resident sociologist in that prison. But he could never get it published because it was, for that time (the era of "treatment and corrections") _politically incorrect_ to advocate firm discipline and control in a prison. Some of the leading university presses, advised by liberal academics, rejected the manuscript. Kantrowitz has now revised the book to bring it into line with the latest writings on "corrections" — though the history and analysis itself is largely as it was written 30 years ago. ISBN. 0911577319 (Paper) $21.50. ISBN: 0911577319 (Hardcover text): Est. $52,00. Release Date: September, 1996.

CONTENTS: Biography of a Book. Preface. 1 The Accidental Observer. 2 Chicago Crime, Politics, and Joseph Ragen's Career. 3 What Do we know of Prison Control? 4 The Round of Life: Controlling Time and Space. 5 Control of Guards. 6 Assignments Essential to Security. 7 All Other Assignments. 8 Control of Inmates. 9. Beatings and Violence. 10. Other than Violence. 11 The Inmate Economy. 12 Conclusion: What of the Future?

RECOMMENDED:Anyone interested in prisons, punishment and corrections should read this revealing book. It is also written in a lucid style, making it an excellent text for use in upper division undergraduate and graduate classes.

Justice with Prejudice:
Race and Criminal Justice in America

Edited by Michael J. Lynch and E. Britt Patterson

IN A FEW WORDS: Extends the articles collected in the widely adopted classic *Race and Criminal Justice*. Emphasis in this volume is on the theoretical and qualitative aspects of the topic. Develops a more profound analysis of the concepts of racism, racial bias and racial discrimination in the criminal justice setting.

CONTENTS: Editor's Preface viii. 1. Thinking About Race and Criminal Justice *Michael J. Lynch and E. Britt Patterson* 2.MoralPanicsIdeology: Drugs,Violence,Race and Punishment in America *Theodore Chiricos* 3. The "Tangle of Pathology" and the Lower Class African-American Family: Historical and Social Science Perspectives *Frankie Y. Bailey 4.* The Image of Black Women in Criminology: Historical Stereotypes as Theoretical Foundation *Jacklyn Huey and Michael J. Lynch 5.* Race, Popular Culture and the News *Lenny Krzycki* 6. Vice and Social Control: Predispositional Detention and the Juvenile Drug Offender *E. Britt Patterson and Laura Davidson Patterson 7.* Race, Contextual Factors, and the Waiver Decision within Juvenile Court Proceedings: Preliminary Findings From a Test of The Symbolic Threat Thesis *Michael J. Leiber, E. Michele Roudebush and Anne C. Woodrick 8.* Race and Criminal Justice: Employment of Minorities in the Criminal Justice System *Mahesh K. Nalla and Charles Corley 9.* Race and Social Class in the Examination of Punishment *Michael Welch.* Bibliography. Index. 200 pages. ISBN 0-911577-34-3. Paper. $21.50. Available September, 1996.

RECOMMENDED: Undergraduate and graduate classes on race relations, race and criminal justice, minorities and criminal justice, feminist studies.